BREAD

Global Baker

Dean Brettschneider

Photography by Aaron McLean

jacqui
small

To my son Jason – thanks for your ongoing support and for all the little things you do behind the scenes that no one knows about. Love, Dad x

First published in the UK and US in 2014 by:
Jacqui Small LLP
An imprint of Aurum Press
74–77 White Lion Street
London N1 9PF

First published by Penguin Group (NZ), 2014

Designed and typeset by Sarah Healey, © Penguin Group (NZ)
Author photograph on page 208 by Claus Peuckert
Prepress by Image Centre Ltd

ISBN 978 1 909342 77 4

A catalogue record for this book is available from the British Library.

2016 2015 2014
10 9 8 7 6 5 4 3 2 1

Printed in China by 1010 Printing

Note the following international terms used in this book:

Proved = Risen
Knocked back = Punched down
Self-raising flour = Self-rising flour

Contents

Introduction

Passion is my main ingredient; it's what makes my breads different from everyone else's. It is something you either have or don't have – you can't be taught passion! I look at young bakers – I take a long look into their eyes, listen to the way they talk and watch how they work with their hands – then I know if they have what it takes to be a successful baker.

Baking, and bread baking in particular, is about the 'feel' or the 'touch'. It's about weighing the ingredients precisely, knowing when the dough is correctly developed or mixed, when it's ready to be knocked back, what shape and how loosely or tightly to mould your loaf, when it's proved or risen correctly, when to cut or slash the loaf and at what angle, what decoration is needed pre- or post-bake, how long to bake it and, finally, when it is baked.

This book is a statement of where bread baking is at today in the food world, how important it is as a mealtime experience, how it brings people together. I want to bring you the very best of my global bread baking influences, adding my 'new world baking' twists to the classics and to other breads to give them a new lease of life. At the same time, I want to give you the knowledge of how to make great breads using an in-depth understanding of ingredients, equipment, process, know-how and techniques.

My very first insight into the world of bread was when my nana taught me how to make scones – a basic quick bread. 'It's all about how you handle the dough,' she told me. 'That's what makes a great scone.' This was my introduction to making bread, and the beginning of a long journey in understanding the science behind what is in effect four simple ingredients that go into making real bread: flour, salt, yeast and water.

In my early days as an apprentice baker I was always inquisitive as to why we did things in a certain way. That trait is still with me today – I'm always questioning the obvious. Some people look at me strangely when I put a piece of raw dough in my mouth and swirl it around as though I'm tasting a particular wine, trying to work out the flavours, textures and so on.

Taste is everything. Even at the beginning of the dough forming, you can tell what's going on. Is it too salty or not salty enough? (Both will cause fermentation problems.) Is it sweet? (If so, I know I will need to handle the dough differently – it will be more delicate in structure, and the baking time will be shorter and temperatures lower.) Does the dough contain a lot of fats? (It will be less tolerant during final proving, and will be denser and shorter in eating qualities.)

Baking is both an art and a science. If you want to get the very best results from your dough, you must give it your very best. Never demand or punish your bread dough; always guide it with a gentle but firm hand, and you will be amazed at the results you achieve.

Another key attribute to becoming a great baker is to seek expert advice when at all possible – then take this advice and put it into practice.

What *is* bread actually? As discussed above, the basic ingredients are flour, salt, yeast and water. Once you have mastered the basics of a good white loaf, then you are ready to explore the many different kinds of breads that are out there – breads from different cultures, with different ingredients, different shapes, baked using different methods, and to suit different dining and eating experiences.

If you want to make great bread, read and understand, read again, practise, make notes, practise some more – and then you are on your way to becoming a great bread baker.

Why not perfect a simple scone first: understand what you are trying to achieve by not mixing the protein strands, then try that same scone again by mixing the dough for five minutes and see what happens. You will be amazed at the difference it makes (not for the better, I might add!). Then use the knowledge and experience you have gained and move on to your next loaf. Eventually you will have the confidence to make that pain au levain (sourdough) or ciabatta you've dreamed of making!

That brings me to the subject of 'less is more': less of the right sort of kneading often means more in terms of finished baked quality. Notice I said 'the right sort of kneading' – learn the correct kneading technique and you will be amazed at the quality, lightness, volume, flavour, crust and crumb of your bread.

In my younger years of learning bread making, particularly when I travelled to do my OE (overseas experience) in the UK and Europe, I chose to work in supermarket instore bakeries, where often frozen pre-formed dough was used, pre-mixes were everywhere, and the only thing that mattered was how fast you could get the dough from mixer to oven and on the shelf. What people forget is that no matter what part of the process is done by others, it's usually still up to the baker to use their judgment, understanding, skill and passion to make an exceptional loaf of bread. I have worked in industrial plant bakeries where 12,000 loaves of bread an hour are produced using high-speed mixing and ingredients that help improve the dough for machinability, or help keep the bread fresher longer. Often the bakers in these factories don't touch the dough with their hands; they just adjust knobs and switches. All this is fascinating – but when you put your baker's hat on, you still have to use your knowledge, understanding and the art of a baker to make key decisions. I won't lie to you and say these types of bakeries and loaves are not real and not good for you – they have their place in the market. One of my jobs is to help these companies to use their processes and equipment to make better bread.

There have been many influential people in my baking life so far. I remember when I was sixteen years old visiting the Holy Grail of French baking in Paris: Poilâne Boulangerie. I was mesmerised by the famous Pain Poilâne that stood in the window, by the simplicity of using natural wild yeast starters, and by the bread stonebaked in a wood-fired oven. Simplicity at its best, I say. Over the years, people such as my good friend and the 'grandfather' of fusion cooking, Peter Gordon, have inspired me to go beyond the normal combining of techniques and flavours wherever possible. Rick Stein gave me the autonomy to work with his bakers and chefs in his Padstow businesses to help them produce better bread with real passion. And then there is my lifelong friend, Richard Bertinet, who almost twenty-five years ago taught me the art of French boulangerie, not to mention how to have fun while making great bread.

Today I head up a very successful artisan bakery business called Baker & Cook; our tag line is

Passion is our main ingredient. Much of what we produce there daily is a reflection of what I consider to be the very best of new world artisan baking. We follow the basic principles, rules and procedures. Baking is actually rather easy; it's only a lack of understanding and knowledge that complicates it.

There are many recipes in this book that reflect all levels of bread baking. Some – such as the quick breads – are simple; others – like building your own wild sourdough culture and creating that elusive pain au levain – are more complicated. I have tried to include recipes that you can share, you can enjoy making, and most of all you can enjoy eating – by yourself or with friends over a glass of wine, with morning coffee or with a wonderful homemade meal.

You will find recipes for bread for all occasions – healthy, savoury, sweet, festive, quick bread, and even breads and dishes that are not really breads but that contain yeast and are fermented, so in my world they are breads.

As a good friend of mine once said, 'Bread is the new coffee.' I hope you enjoy baking the many breads in this book. But equally, I hope you indulge in the tips, techniques and knowledge that I have shared to give you a better understanding and appreciation of baking bread.

Bake well,
Dean

A History of Bread Making

Baking is one of the oldest crafts in history. According to some, bread making has been around, in its simplest form, for 30,000 years; and relics of bread making have been found in ancient Egyptian tombs. One theory is that bread making began with primitive man grinding edible grains between two large stones, mixing the resultant meal with water and baking it on hot stones. This was a very simple and natural process, and more of a cooking technique than a baking one, which requires an enclosed oven chamber. Another well-founded theory has it that bread making in earnest goes back to 8000 BC. This type of early bread was referred to as 'flat bread' because there was no leavening ingredient such as yeast to allow fermentation to take place. The bread was dense in texture, had a dark crumb and was not easy to digest. One could imagine it would have been rather flavourless, too. Nonetheless these flat breads, or unleavened breads, formed a big part of the daily diet.

In its most primitive form, bread making was reliant on a very small number of natural ingredients and crude tools. It is therefore not hard to deduce that traditional bread making was time-consuming and somewhat physical – it was done out of necessity, for survival. It is also evident it was not an exact science, and experimentation with bread making has continued throughout the ages.

Bread making is said to have spread from areas along the Nile in Egypt, finding its way into all parts of Europe. In medieval times, in particular in Europe, bread was not only considered a staple part of the diet but was also used as a vessel to eat from; a stale piece of bread was often used as a plate, and called a 'trencher', which was eaten at the end of the meal.

If there was one key event that contributed to the improvement of the eating and keeping properties of bread, it was the ability to ferment bread dough. Archaeological evidence shows that the Egyptians made leavened bread as early as 4000 BC, after the discovery that yeast spores, when they came into contact with other ingredients in bread dough, would stimulate a natural fermentation process. It is likely this was discovered by accident, when some older dough was mixed through some freshly made dough. Legend has it that a slave in one of the royal households forgot about some dough he had put aside and, on returning, found it had almost doubled in size. Attempting to hide his mistake, the slave beat down the bread and baked it, and also added it to freshly prepared dough, in effect creating a 'starter'. The resulting bread was found to be lighter and to have superior eating qualities.

Since its invention, bread has been considered a part of the staple diet – the 'staff of life' – and an essential and readily available communal commodity. The importance that bread played in the formation of early human societies cannot be underestimated. Records show that from the western half of Asia, where wheat was first domesticated, cultivation spread north and west to encompass Europe and Africa. This enabled humans to become farmers of the land rather than having to be reliant on hunting and foraging for food. This went hand in hand with the formation of communities.

The skill, craft and art of the baker was admired in these communities – and so the baking trade came to be considered one of the most noble crafts, with bakers enjoying special privileges for the part they played in the community. The 'artisan baker' has been a time-honoured profession, and most cultures have developed their own iconic breads, reflecting their traditional values and beliefs.

At times baking became a heavily regulated occupation, because bread was such a vital part of the daily diet. In England in 1266 a law was passed for the regulation of bread prices, and this remained in force for 600 years; and there are examples of medieval laws where the baker was subjected to fines, imprisonment and even corporal punishment if he broke the law.

One element of bread making was common to all techniques and recipes: heat. The first loaves of bread (called 'cakes') were apparently baked in the sun; later they were baked on heated rocks or in the embers of an earth oven. Archaeologists will often look for the remnants of earth ovens (both the structure and the contents) on their digs, as this can help to identify what foods were consumed at the time. From at least the nineteenth century on, breads were baked in wood-fired ovens. The Egyptians placed the bread dough in a clay pot and, when the bread was baked, they would break the clay pot open to release it. This is one of the earliest records of bread being baked in a container, giving loaves a common shape.

The most common means for heating the baking chambers was from below: this was another skill that the baker acquired. During the Middle Ages it was not uncommon for each community or landlord to have their own oven. Households would bring their dough and the baker would bake it. As time progressed, the baker began to make his own goods to sell: by the fifth century BC, bread was sold in the markets of Athens and in bakers' shops in Rome.

These days, after much experimentation, bread making is a more exact science. But the basic principles remain the same – and the baker is still a craftsperson, creating an essential staple of the modern diet.

Paul Hansen, Baker

Ingredients

Wheat flour

Wheat flour is the most important ingredient in the bakery. It provides bulk and structure to most baked products, including breads, cakes, biscuits (cookies) and pastries. There are many different types of flour and each has been developed with a particular baked product in mind.

Flour is obtained from the cereal wheat. A grain of wheat consists of six main parts, but for baking the endosperm, bran and germ are the most important.

The endosperm is the white part of the wheat grain from which white flour is milled once the bran and germ has been removed. It consists largely of:
- tightly packed starch granules
- soluble proteins (albumens)
- insoluble gluten-forming proteins (glutenin and gliadin)
- oil
- moisture
- mineral matter.

Bran is the outside skin of the wheat grain. It consists of six main layers that provide protection, colour and enzymes. The bran is largely removed during the milling process to make white flour. It is blended back into the finely ground endosperm (white flour) to produce wheatmeal or brown flour.

The germ is the embryo of the wheat grain in which most of the vitamins and minerals are stored. It is largely removed in the milling of white flour because the oil it contains soon becomes rancid and the enzymes it produces have a detrimental influence on the fermentation process in bread making.

The germ, which is blended back into the endosperm and bran to produce wholemeal (whole wheat) flour, is rich in:
- oil
- calcium
- vitamin B
- enzymes.

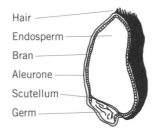

The composition of flour will naturally be similar to that of the wheat it is milled from. An average composition would be as follows.

Constituent	Strong flour %	Soft flour %
Starch	70	72
Insoluble gluten-forming proteins	11–13	8
Moisture	12–15	12–15
Sugar	2.5	2.5
Oil	1–1.5	1–1.5
Soluble proteins	1	1

Extraction rate is the term used to determine the amount of flour obtained from the wheat after the milling process. Wholemeal (or whole wheat) has a 100 per cent extraction rate; white flour is around 78 per cent; and pastry flours, which need to have whiter, speck-free particles, are often around 60 per cent.

The insoluble gluten-forming proteins present in flour are known as gluten. Gluten is made up of two different proteins called glutenin and gliadin, each of which has different characteristics. Glutenin produces elastic properties while gliadin produces extensible (stretching) properties. Gluten is produced in a bread dough, for example, when water has been added and the dough has been mixed sufficiently to develop the gluten. The suitability of a flour for bakery products is determined by the quality of the gluten and, in some cases, the quantity of gluten present. Flour that contains a good quality (and a lot of) gluten is known as strong flour; flour that contains a lower quality (and less) gluten is known as soft flour.

You can gauge the strength of a flour by squeezing it tightly in one hand. A soft (or weak) flour will cling and clump together and feels very smooth when the hand is opened. A strong (or bread) flour will crumble again into a powder and will feel slightly coarse when rubbed between two fingers.

Hand test for flour strength. The hand on the left holds a soft (plain) flour, used for cakes, biscuits, sweet and short pastry; the hand on the right holds a strong (bread) flour, used in breads, yeast-raised products and puff pastry.

Flour, grain and meal should be stored in cool, dry conditions. White flours are best used within 6 months; wholemeal or whole wheat flours should be used within 3–4 months.

Types of flour

A wide variety of flour is milled from wheat and other grains for use in baking. Here are the most common types of flour.

+ **Strong (bread) flour** contains a high level of gluten, which is beneficial in making bread, yeast-raised products and puff pastry.
+ **Plain (all-purpose) flour** is a medium-strength flour used in making short-pastry products and baking powder-aerated products such as scones, muffins, biscuits (cookies) and slices.

+ **Self-raising flour** is a medium-strength flour that has been blended with baking powder, which makes up about 6 per cent of the volume. It is used for batters, scones, pikelets and cakes. You can make your own self-raising flour by sifting together 300g (2 cups) plain (all-purpose) flour and 3 teaspoons baking powder at least seven times.

+ **Wholemeal (whole wheat) flour** is milled from the whole wheat grain and so contains the bran and germ. It is suitable for all bread and yeast-raised products, pastries, cakes and biscuits (cookies). Bran acts like tiny pieces of glass within an unbaked product; it cuts and damages the gluten network that has been developed to give strength, structure and volume to the finished baked product. Recipes using wholemeal (whole wheat) flour make allowances for this, for example by adding extra gluten flour (2 per cent of flour weight) and by slightly increasing the water content (approximately 3 per cent of flour weight).

+ **Rye flour** is the third most common flour after plain and wholemeal (whole wheat) flour. Although rye flour contains some flour proteins, these proteins do not form gluten. Therefore, breads made from 100 per cent rye flour will be sticky at the dough stage and heavy and dense after baking. Rye breads are by far the most popular breads in Germany and Eastern Europe.

+ **Semolina flour** is coarsely ground endosperm (white flour), used for thickening pie fillings, dusting the baker's peel (see page 26) for ease of transferring the breads onto the oven hearth, and as an ingredient in crusty breads.

+ **Cornflour** (or cornstarch) is obtained from kernels of corn or maize. It is almost 100 per cent starch and does not contain any insoluble gluten-forming proteins. Cornflour (cornstarch) is used mainly as a thickening agent for custards, sauces and fillings.

+ **Rice flour** is obtained from the cereal rice. It is almost 100 per cent starch and does not contain any insoluble gluten-forming proteins. It is added to cake recipes and biscuits (cookies); this assists in absorbing the liquids for either keeping qualities or crispness properties, e.g. shortbread.

+ **Soy flour** is obtained from soybeans. It is very rich in protein, but does not contain any insoluble gluten-forming proteins. It is very high in fat, making it an excellent ingredient for any bread recipe that requires keeping qualities, an even texture or increased volume.

+ **Malt flour** and other malt products are obtained from barley or wheat that has undergone a controlled process known as malting, which begins after the grains have been cleaned. Germination takes place in a temperature- and humidity-controlled environment. During this period, the starch within the grain is converted into simple sugars. This process is halted when the grains are heated during the drying stages of the process. Malt is an important food source for yeast in yeasted dough.

When enzyme-active malt flour is added to a bread dough, the natural enzymes in the malt flour break down starch to produce maltose and other sugars which act as yeast foods, enhancing yeast performance during fermentation. These sugars, in combination with the protein in bread flour, also form browning compounds through caramelisation and Maillard reactions, providing crust colour without excessive baking. These characteristics make high-malt flours ideal for the production of sourdoughs, crusty breads and cracker-type biscuits.

+ **Cornmeal** (or polenta) is made from kernels of corn or maize, ground to a fine, medium or coarse

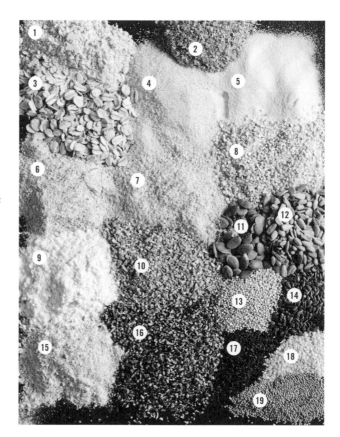

1. Gluten flour
2. Wheat bran
3. Rolled oats
4. Cornmeal polenta
5. Semolina
6. Rye meal flour
7. Wheatgerm
8. Barley
9. White flour
10. Kibbled wheat
11. Pumpkin seeds
12. Sunflower seeds
13. Quinoa seed
14. Flaxseed/Linseed
15. Wholemeal (whole wheat) flour
16. Kibbled purple wheat
17. Black sesame seeds
18. White sesame seeds
19. Chia seed

texture. It is used in products such as cornbread and pasta, or it can be cooked and eaten by itself.

+ **Organic flour** is milled from organically grown wheat. Most baked products can be made using organic flours, although the quality of the baked product can sometimes vary.

+ **Spelt flour** is made from the spelt grain, found by archaeologists in prehistoric sites. It comes from the same family as wheat but has a different genetic structure and is higher in protein, vitamins and minerals. Some people with wheat allergies may be able to tolerate spelt products. Today spelt is grown commercially and makes marvellous bread with a rich, nutty flavour.

+ **Grains:** many types of flour are also available in wholegrain or kibbled (cut) grain forms. The coarser flours are used when making wholegrain or multicereal breads, but the grains needs soaking for at least 12 hours in equal quantities of water and grain in order to soften them before use.

Salt

Salt is a natural mineral found in many parts of the world. It comes in many different forms: table salt, iodised salt, sea salt and rock salt. When used in baking, it is more than just a flavour or seasoning enhancer. It also performs these functions:

+ strengthens the gluten structure of the dough and makes it more stretchable
+ controls the rate of fermentation of yeast-raised doughs
+ improves crust and crumb colour and stability
+ increases shelf life.

Salt is hygroscopic and should be stored away from moisture.

Sugar

Sugar is obtained from two sources: sugar cane and sugar beet. It is refined to produce many different types, including white sugar, brown sugar, raw sugar, Demerara sugar and icing (confectioners') sugar. Sugar also takes the form of a syrup, such as molasses, treacle (blackstrap molasses), honey and glucose.

Sugar possesses the following properties:

+ sweetness
+ flavour
+ creates tenderness and fineness of texture by weakening (shortening) the gluten structure
+ caramelises during baking to give crust colour
+ acts as a creaming agent with butter and a foaming agent with eggs
+ acts as a source of food for yeast during fermentation
+ improves shelf life by retaining and attracting moisture.

Icing (confectioners') sugar is sugar ground to a powder with starch added.

Nibbed sugar is in the form of large crystals, similar to rock salt, and is used for decorating baked products.

Eggs

A whole egg consists of a yolk, a white and a shell. Egg whites are known as albumen. The size of the eggs can have an effect on a recipe, so it is often necessary to weigh eggs – after they are cracked.

Composition of an average egg

	Whole egg %	White (albumen) %	Yolk %
Water	73	86	49
Protein	13	12	17
Fat	12	–	32
Minerals	2	2	2

Eggs have the following properties when used in baking:

+ add moisture

- improve shelf life by moisturising, emulsifying, enriching and shortening baked products
- provide structure: when subjected to heat during the baking process, eggs will expand, the proteins are set and the structure is established
- emulsify: egg yolk contains lecithin, a natural emulsifier agent, which assists in combining two substances or ingredients that normally do not mix that well together, e.g. water and fat
- enrich: eggs contain high levels of protein and fat, which add to the nutritional value
- add flavour and colour
- glaze: mixed with milk or water, eggs give a shine to baked goods.

A small egg, when cracked, weighs approximately 50g/2oz (30g/1oz white and 20g/¾oz yolk), a medium egg weighs 53–63g/2–2¼oz and a large egg weighs 63–73g/2–2½oz.

Milk

Whole milk is fresh milk with nothing added or removed. It contains 3.5 per cent milk fat, 8.5 per cent non-fat milk solids and 88 per cent water. Fresh milk should always be kept in the refrigerator and the use-by date adhered to. Milk is also processed into different forms, such as milk powder, condensed milk and evaporated milk. It is used in baking to add moistness, texture, colour, shelf life and nutritional value.

Cream

Fresh cream is obtained from the fat content of cow's milk. It is not often used as a liquid in doughs or batters, except in a few specialty products; however, it is used in fillings and toppings. When whipped correctly, cream should double in volume. Always store cream at 0–4°C (32–39.2°F).

Butter

Butter guarantees a top-quality baking product. It has a low melting point and therefore melts very early in the baking process. Some recipes call for chilled, softened or even melted butter, and it is important to follow the recipe for a good-quality finished product.

Baking powder

Baking powder is a mixture of an acid (cream of tartar) and an alkali (bicarbonate of soda/baking soda). It is responsible for the aeration, final volume and, often, crumb structure of a product. When baking powder becomes moist during the mixing process and is then heated in the oven, there is a reaction between the acid and alkali, which produces a gas (carbon dioxide). The gas lifts and pushes up the final product until the proteins from the eggs and flour have set during baking. All batters and doughs containing baking powder should be kept cool (21°C/70°F or below) and prepared quickly to prevent the gas from forming before the mixture enters the oven.

Nuts

All nuts have a limited shelf life because of their high fat content and can turn rancid in a very short time if not stored correctly. Keep them in a cool place and, if purchased in large quantities, they should be stored in the freezer until needed. When using nuts in a bread dough, combine them with the dough towards the end of mixing. This is done for two reasons: first so they do not break up too much; and second because, as a result of breaking up, nuts release oil which will have a softening effect on the dough, making it difficult to handle.

Below is a list of nuts commonly used in baking.

- **Almonds** can be used whole with skins on, blanched, split, flaked, nibbed or ground.
- **Walnuts** are used either as pieces or whole for decoration, or chopped and added to doughs and batters.

- **Pecans** are generally used in premium goods because of the high cost.
- **Coconut** is used as a coating or decoration on sweet breads and other baked goods.
- **Hazelnuts** are best if lightly roasted first; they have a distinctive sweet flavour.

Dried fruit

Currants, sultanas (golden raisins), raisins, mixed peel, figs, dates and apricots are the most commonly available dried fruit, but you can also find dried peaches, apples, bananas, and so on. All are suitable for adding to dough, batter mixtures and fillings. When using dried fruits in a bread dough, mix them in towards the end of mixing. This is done for two reasons: first so they do not break up too much; and second because dried fruits contain sugar which, when released, will cause the yeast to be over-fed and to work slowly, resulting in excessive fermentation and rising times. Dried fruit is prepared by washing, drying, cleaning, removing stones and stalks, and soaking in water or alcohol to moisten the fruit.

Cocoa

Cocoa is the dry powder that remains after part of the cocoa butter is removed from chocolate liquor. Cocoa contains starch, which tends to absorb moisture in a cake batter; therefore when cocoa powder is added to a batter a reduction in the amount of flour is necessary to keep the recipe balanced. Using cocoa in a bread dough is fine, but a maximum of 10 per cent of flour weight is recommended. Dutch cocoa is further processed to neutralise the natural acidity of cocoa.

Chocolate

Chocolate couverture is prepared by milling together cocoa butter, cocoa and sugar. It is expensive and is usually used when producing top-quality, high-class chocolate products. Couverture needs tempering before use, to ensure that the cocoa-butter crystals stay suspended in the cocoa solids. To temper chocolate couverture, follow these steps.

1. Half fill a saucepan with cold water, bring to the boil and remove from the heat.

2. Break chocolate couverture into small pieces and place in a stainless steel bowl that will fit inside the saucepan of water. Place the bowl of chocolate in the saucepan of hot water. Never allow any water or steam to come into contact with the chocolate as this will cause it to thicken and become unstable.

3. Stir the chocolate with a clean wooden spoon until it has reached 40°C (104°F) and the chocolate has melted. You may need to remove the bowl from the water from time to time to avoid overheating the chocolate.

4. Tip two-thirds of the chocolate onto a marble slab or cold, clean work surface. Using two palette knives, rotate the chocolate (mix it in a backwards and forwards motion) until it has cooled to 37°C (98.6°F) (about blood temperature).

5. Place the cooled chocolate back in the bowl with the other third and mix thoroughly until well combined.

6. Place the bowl back in the warm water and warm the chocolate couverture to exactly 30°C (86°F). Always use at this temperature and you will achieve a nice sheen on the chocolate once it has set.

Chocolate compound – or chocolate coating – is prepared from vegetable fats, cocoa powder, sugar, milk solids and emulsifiers. It is much easier to use than couverture and does not require any special preparation. It is available in dark, milk and white. To melt chocolate compound, follow the steps overleaf.

1. Half fill a saucepan with cold water, bring to the boil and remove from the heat.

2. Break chocolate into small pieces and place in a stainless steel bowl that will fit inside the saucepan of water. Place the bowl of chocolate in the hot water. Never allow any water or steam to come into contact with the chocolate as this will cause the chocolate to thicken and become unusable.

3. Stir the chocolate with a clean wooden spoon until it has reached 40°C (104°F) and the chocolate has melted. You may need to remove the bowl from the water from time to time to avoid overheating the chocolate.

4. Use chocolate compound at 40°C (104°F) to achieve a nice sheen once the chocolate has set.

Spices

Spices are aromatic or pungent vegetable substances used to flavour food. They are obtained from various parts of different plants:

- bark – cinnamon, cassia
- buds – cloves
- flowers – rose and orange blossom
- fruit – aniseed, peppers
- leaves – sage, thyme
- root – ginger
- seeds – nutmeg, sesame, poppy and caraway
- stem – angelica.

Spices can be used in their whole or ground form, but the ground form loses its flavour rapidly and should be replaced after 6 months. Spices should be used in moderation in baked goods; too much can make the product inedible. Spices have a retarding effect on yeast activity, so when using them in yeast-raised products (for example hot cross buns), increase the yeast by 0.5–1 per cent of flour weight.

Vanilla extract

Vanilla extract is a solution containing the flavour compound vanillin as the primary ingredient. Pure vanilla extract is made by macerating and percolating vanilla pods (beans) in a solution of ethyl alcohol and water. It comes with or without seeds. It is the most used flavour in baking and is a wonderful addition in many foods.

Guar gum or xanthan gum

Guar gum is made from the seeds of the guar bean and is used to absorb large amounts of water. You can also use xanthan gum. Both are available from local health-food shops and are totally natural.

Yeast

Yeast is a living single-cell microorganism that can only be seen under the microscope. The strain used by commercial bakers is called *Saccharomyces cerevisiae*. Yeast is responsible for volume in bread, buns, rolls, croissants, Danish pastries and similar products. The activity of yeast in dough is called fermentation. This is the process by which yeast acts on sugars and changes them into carbon dioxide and alcohol. The release of gas produces the rising action – also known as leavening – in yeast-raised products. The alcohol evaporates during and immediately after baking. For yeast to produce carbon dioxide and alcohol, it requires time to ferment; moisture to survive and grow; warmth – the ideal temperature is 28–32°C (82–90°F); and a food source – e.g. sugar. Without these the yeast cells will die and the result will be an inferior product.

Effects of different ingredients and temperatures on yeast are:

- Salt slows down the activity of yeast. A small amount of salt (1.8–2 per cent of flour weight) can be used to control fermentation; however, excessive amounts of salt will retard or even kill the yeast cells. Never mix salt directly with yeast, because of salt's hygroscopic properties – it will draw moisture from the yeast cells.

+ Sugar is a food source for yeast. If excessive amounts of sugar are added, however, it will slow down the activity of yeast; in some cases – e.g. for sweet doughs, Danish pastries and brioches – extra yeast needs to be added to compensate for the effects of the sugar.
+ Fats used at high levels will slow down the activity of yeast.
+ The correct temperature is crucial for healthy yeast activity. Optimum temperature is 28–32°C (82–90°F). If the temperature is 0°C (32°F) and below, the yeast cells will die; at 0–10°C (32–50°F) yeast activity will slow down or cease; at 32–45°C (90–113°F) yeast activity will become excessive and incontrollable; and at 45–60°C (113–140°F) yeast activity will stop and the yeast cells will be destroyed.

Fresh yeast or compressed yeast can be found at select supermarkets and delicatessens. It has a limited shelf life and cannot be frozen.

Instant dry yeast can be purchased from the supermarket. It has an excellent shelf life if unopened. When using instant dry yeast in place of fresh yeast, use one-third; for example, if a recipe requires 15g (5 tsp) fresh yeast, use 5g (1¼ tsp) instant dry yeast.

Instant dry yeast does not need to be added to water before use; simply add it to the flour and mix through.

Active dry yeast is encapsulated and looks like very small balls or granules. It must be hydrated in water before using, to dissolve the encapsulated outer surface.

Instant dry yeast (left) and fresh compressed yeast (right).

Water

Water is an essential ingredient in bread making for several reasons.

+ It hydrates the flour proteins to produce gluten, which gives dough structure and retains the gas produced by yeast.
+ It helps the dispersion of salt and sugar, because yeast can only absorb food that is in solution.
+ It plays an important part in the final finished dough temperature (FDT), which is controlled by the experienced baker. Different doughs require a different FDT. Sourdough, for example, requires an FDT of 24–26°C (75–79°F), as it needs a slow fermentation process. A sweet bun might require an FDT of 28–30°C (82–86°F) and a shorter fermentation.
+ The correct amount of water helps to increase the shelf life of a baked loaf. Approximately 12 per cent of water evaporates off during the baking process.

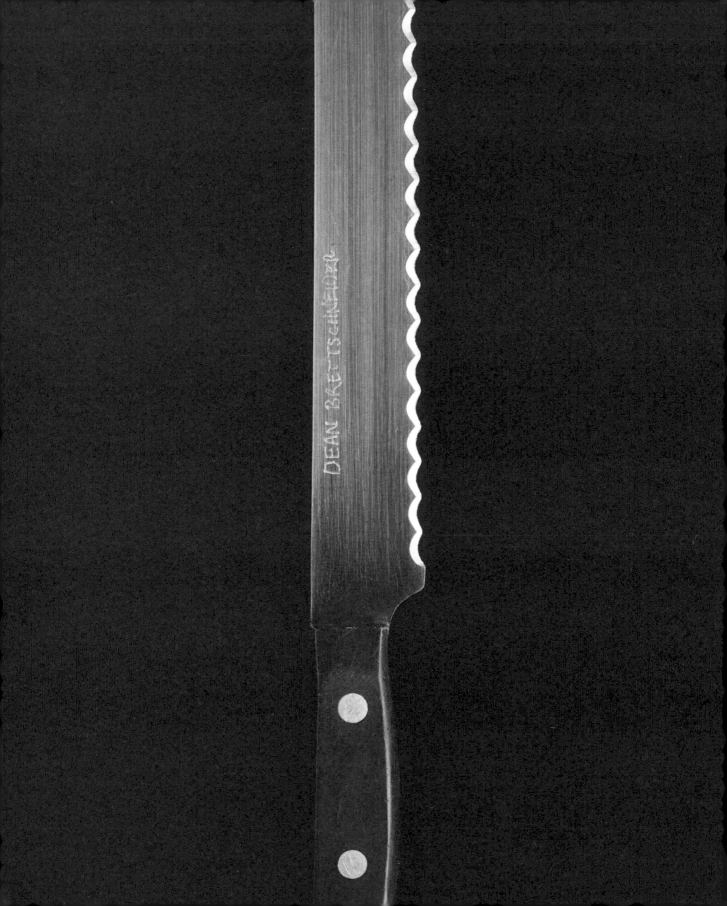

Equipment

Your hands

These are the two most important pieces of equipment that you should have in your 'toolbox'. Your hands must be strong and firm, yet gentle and sensitive; able to feel when the dough is fully mixed, elastic and at the same time smooth and silky to the touch; as well as being light and delicate enough to gently fold and lift the softest of flours through a perfectly aerated batter.

You need to have a good feeling for temperature and consistency when using your hands. By making the same recipe more than once, you will develop the 'baker's feel' and know when it feels right to stop folding the flour into your delicate light-as-air sponge or when to put the loaf of bread in the oven, and you will be able to tell if your product is under-baked, perfectly baked or over-baked.

I often see people working with scrapers, mixers, spoons and knives, afraid to touch the dough because they will get their hands messy and dirty. Go on, get right in there, and don't underestimate the value of using your hands in baking!

Scales

As with all recipes, the more accurately you measure the more chance you have of gaining perfect results. A good set of digital scales is one of the best pieces of baking equipment you can have. Treat them well and you will have them for many, many years. I recommend digital scales with 1-gram increments.

Measuring cups and spoons

Some measurements are given in cups and spoons as well as in metric measurements. Always keep a set of these handy when doing recipe development: weigh the ingredients, record the weight and refer to it next time, to keep consistency in your baking.

Mixing bowls

Always have on hand a range of mixing bowls for different purposes, from a very large earthenware bowl for mixing dough to small glass bowls for weighing individual ingredients.

Electric mixer

If you have a mixer, by all means use it; but if not, all of the breads in this book can be made by hand.

Dough scraper or cutter

This is a rectangle of stainless steel with a cutting edge and a rolled steel or wooden handle. It can also be made from a sturdy rectangle of plastic. The dough scraper is used to cut or divide dough into pieces, and to scrape up excess dough sticking to the work surface. More flexible plastic scrapers can also be used for scraping down the sides of a mixing bowl.

Proofing basket.

Rolling pin.

Proofing cloth.

Proofing baskets

Proofing baskets are either a close-woven basket made from coiled cane for German-style breads, or a cane basket lined with a linen cloth for French-style breads; both kinds are available from specialty cook shops. Dust the proofing basket with a good coating of flour before putting the dough into the basket to prove. Once the loaf has risen to the required size, invert it onto the baking tray or baking stone.

Alternatively, place a tea towel inside a bowl and dust it well with flour.

Rolling pin

Use a heavy wooden rolling pin, at least 30–40cm (12–16in) in length, when doing final dough shaping for certain kinds of breads, such as croissants, Danish pastries, hamburger buns, Chelsea buns or cinnamon rolls.

Proofing cloths and dough covers

Dough is a living organism, and needs to be kept warm. Cover your dough with a light cloth such as a tea (dish) towel, or with a sheet of strong plastic such as a clean supermarket bag, to prevent the dough from getting cold and to keep the yeast working at a good pace. Covering the dough also prevents it from forming a dry outer skin or crust.

You can also use a heavier cloth, made from canvas or Belgian linen; this is known as a proofing cloth or couche. Dust the cloth well with flour, then gather it around the dough piece to help hold the shape of the loaf or baguette and to protect it from drying out on the sides and bottom during proof and fermentation times. Once the dough has risen to its final size, gently lift it from the floured cloth onto a baker's peel (see page 26) and transfer it to the baking tray or baking stone.

Thermometers

Digital thermometer: use a digital thermometer to get accurate temperature readings of your ingredients and the environment. This is particularly important when dealing with yeast-raised products, as yeast is a living organism and requires a consistent temperature to produce carbon dioxide and alcohol.

Oven thermometer: always have a good oven thermometer to place in different parts of the oven so you have a clear idea of what temperature the oven really is.

Proofing cabinet

A proofing cabinet, or prover, is a warm chamber that is set at optimum temperature and humidity for proofing dough. If you do not have a prover, place

Alternative to a proofing cabinet.

Baking tins and trays.

Fine mesh sieve.

your dough for final proof or rising in a warm, draught-free place. Loosely cover the dough with a large sheet of clingfilm (plastic wrap) to prevent a skin or crust from forming on the surface.

Refrigerator

Some bread doughs are put in the refrigerator to slow down (retard) the action of yeast and enable the dough to develop flavour and texture. An example is sourdough, which requires a long, cool fermentation process. Place yeasted dough in the refrigerator after it has had its first rise and knock back, before scaling and final moulding.

Baking tins and trays

Most breads are baked on the hearth of the oven, on a preheated pizza stone (as mentioned below), or in loaf tins (pans); however, some breads and other bakery products are baked on specialty tins (pans) and trays. Always use strong, heavy baking trays (cookie sheets) that hold their heat and are solid.

Line baking trays (cookie sheets), tins (pans) and pizza stones with non-stick baking (parchment) paper first, for ease of baking and turning out.

Baking mats and non-stick baking paper

Non-stick baking mats (usually silicone) and non-stick baking paper are essential for lining baking tins and trays to prevent the baked product from sticking.

Freezer

Freezing raw yeast dough is not advisable, particularly in a domestic freezer with no airflow. The slow freezing causes large ice crystals to form and this kills many of the yeast cells by rupturing the cell wall. Large ice crystals also cut many of the gluten strands that have built up during the kneading process. Both of these actions cause reduced gas production and a weak gluten network that will not retain the carbon dioxide produced; the result will be a small-volume, dense loaf.

Fine mesh sieve

A fine mesh sieve (strainer) is used to dust or sift flour over your proofing cloths and baskets. You can also dust your dough with flour prior to baking so that you can slash the dough with a razor blade or sharp knife.

Serrated knife

Use a serrated knife to cut bread and rolls, as this will give a clean cut without squashing the bread.

Pastry brush.

Baking stone.

Baker's peel.

Pastry brush

A pastry brush has many uses in bread making, for example brushing olive oil on panini and focaccia; glazing the tops of sweet breads with egg wash or sugar glaze; or dusting excess flour off the surface of dough during final moulding and shaping.

Baking stone or pizza stone

Bakers often bake their breads on the oven hearth, which allows the bread to bake the instant you slide the raw dough onto it using a baker's peel (see below) or a flat baking tray (cookie sheet). This gives a solid bake and crust to the baked bread. You can use a pizza stone instead.

Baker's peel

A baker's peel is a long-handled flat shovel used to transfer the dough piece (usually a loaf) directly onto the preheated baking stone. First place the dough piece on a piece of non-stick baking (parchment) paper; then, when the dough is ready to be placed in the oven, slide the peel underneath the baking (parchment) paper, open the oven door and with a quick forward and backward jerk slide the dough piece (baking (parchment) paper and all) onto the baking stone. Of course, before non-stick baking (parchment) paper was invented, the time-honoured way was to first dust the peel with coarse semolina flour or polenta (cornmeal) before placing the loaf on the peel and transferring it to the baking stone. This method results in a crustier bottom, as the semolina will crisp up nicely in the oven.

Oven

There is no need for the home baker to invest thousands of dollars in a state-of-the-art oven – you can easily make a few adjustments to your existing oven, for example, by adding a pan of hot rocks, or spraying with warm water to create steam (see page 27).

Always preheat the oven and, before placing anything in it, check that it has reached the correct temperature. An oven thermometer is useful for this.

Note: all recipes in this book are based on a standard oven. If you are using a fan-assisted oven, reduce the temperatures given in this book by 10–15°C (25°F), and take care as the baking time will also be reduced.

Razor blade or dough-slashing knife

Each loaf or roll may be cut so that it has a planned and predictable place at which to burst and achieve

Dough-slashing knife.

Scissors.

Hot rocks and chain.

the oven spring it needs to develop to its full potential. Use a double-edged razor blade threaded onto a bamboo skewer to give a sharp and precise cut; or use a specialty dough-slashing knife. The cut must be done at the correct time and at the correct angle to prevent the dough from collapsing before being placed into the oven. Slash or cut the bread three-quarters of the way through the final proof stage; if it is done any later, the dough may collapse before it goes into the oven.

Scissors

Instead of slashing or cutting rolls, you can snip the tops with scissors and create peaks that toast nicely in the oven, giving a little extra crunch when eating. As with slashing and cutting, snipping must be done three-quarters of the way through the final proof stage to avoid the dough collapsing before going into the oven.

Hot rocks and chain

The preferred method of creating steam for baking crusty breads. Place rocks (not pebbles) in an oven tray and coil a length of metal chain evenly among the rocks. Preheat in the oven and add water to create steam (see next entry).

Spray bottle

Keep a bottle of water with a spray nozzle handy for spraying the preheated oven to create steam, just before putting bread in the oven to bake (see page 44). A spray can be useful when applying seeds, cheese, etc., to the top of your rolls or loaf before baking, to help the topping stick. Simply spray dough with water and sprinkle topping on. If you notice during the final proofing stage that your dough piece is getting a dry skin and crusting over, lightly spray the surface with warm water to remove the dry crust, which will prevent the dough from rising and achieving its correct volume.

Cooling rack

Always place loaves or rolls to cool on a cooling rack or wire rack; this enables air to circulate around the whole loaf and prevents the bottom from sweating and going soggy.

Bread Know-how

There are 11 basic steps in making and baking breads, which I will explain in detail here. Using this as a guide, you will have all the information you need to bake successful, good-quality breads.

The steps are:
1. Mixing or kneading dough by hand
2. Bulk fermentation (first rising) of dough
3. Knocking back or deflating dough
4. Dividing or scaling dough
5. Rounding or pre-shaping dough
6. Intermediate proof
7. Final moulding and placing on trays
8. Final proof (second rising)
9. Decorating – cutting, seeding and dusting
10. Baking
11. Cooling.

1. Mixing or kneading dough by hand

Mixing or kneading dough should be fun and enjoyable, not something that is hard work or should be hurried. Ensure that you knead on a solid surface with plenty of space and the work surface is of suitable height. The secret to easy hand kneading is to rest the dough for 1–2 minutes regularly during the kneading process. This allows the elastic flour proteins to relax a little before further kneading and manipulation and also, importantly, allows a small rest for yourself. You will find hand kneading much more enjoyable – and not so tiring – when using this method (see images overleaf).

How to tell when dough is fully mixed

Mixing and kneading is one of the most important steps in successful bread making. Good bread flour contains a protein called gluten, which gives structure and strength to all yeast-raised breads.

The protein first absorbs liquid; then, as the dough is mixed or kneaded, the gluten forms long, elastic, rubbery strands known as the gluten network.

As the dough begins to rise, the gluten network captures the gases produced by the yeast in tiny pockets or cells and allows the dough to rise and expand. If the gluten network within the dough has not been correctly developed (mixed), these gases will escape into the air, resulting in a collapsed, small-volume loaf.

There are many factors that determine when a dough is fully mixed:
+ temperature of water – if the water is too cold the dough will take longer to develop; and if the water is too hot the dough will also take too long to develop and it will cause the dough to overheat and the yeast to work too quickly
+ speed of kneading
+ selection and amounts of raw ingredients – doughs that are high in fat or sugar take less time to mix because these ingredients have a 'shortening' and 'softening' effect on the gluten network.

When the dough is ready:
+ the dough has a smooth, silky and elastic texture; a rough and easily broken dough still needs a lot more mixing
+ a piece of dough when stretched has a smooth, satiny sheen, and the dough is elastic and extensible (see stretch test on page 31).

Scan the QR code to view a video on the basics of the bread making techniques mentioned in this chapter.

Place flour in a large bowl and sprinkle other dry ingredients around the flour.

Slowly add water and any other liquids into the middle of the dry ingredients. Always reserve a small amount of water to adjust the dough to correct consistency.

Moving your hands in a circular motion, mix in the liquids to form a cohesive dough mass that has cleared the sides of the bowl.

Once dough has cleared the sides of the bowl, tip it out onto a lightly floured work surface ready for kneading. Have a small bowl of flour handy for lightly dusting the work surface during the kneading process.

To knead dough, using both hands lift dough upwards and then fold it back onto itself. This stretches the dough and traps air in it. Repeat this procedure for 1–2 minutes. Leave dough to rest untouched for 2–3 minutes to allow it to recover and relax. The dough will be sticky and rough in texture at this stage. Don't worry: this will improve, with only minor adjustments in ingredients necessary.

Continue to knead the dough using the method described, alternating kneading and resting, for about 15 minutes.

The dough will become smooth, silky and elastic, with little air trapped inside.

The stretch test

An under-developed dough. Notice the rough and easily broken texture when it is stretched out. The flour proteins (gluten) have not been developed and are not holding in the gas produced by the yeast. The result will be a flat, small, dense loaf of bread.

A correctly developed dough – smooth, elastic and extensible when stretched. The gluten has been fully developed and is retaining the gas produced by the yeast, creating a strong dough. The result will be a healthy, bold loaf of bread.

2. Bulk fermentation of dough

Bulk fermentation – or first rising – describes the length of time that dough is allowed to ferment in bulk, from after the dough has been mixed or kneaded until it is divided into smaller portions. This period can be anywhere from 1 to 18 hours, depending on two factors:

+ the amount of salt and yeast in the recipe
+ the temperature of the dough, which should be 25–26°C (77–79°F).

During bulk fermentation, place the dough in a lightly oiled container large enough to allow the dough to double in size. The dough must be covered to prevent the dough surface from forming a skin. Place the dough in an environment where the temperature will remain constant (e.g. in the hot-water cupboard).

3. Knocking back or deflating dough

During the bulk fermentation period the dough increases in volume – often to double its size. This is due to gases given off by the yeast. To prevent the gases from escaping prematurely, the dough is gently 'knocked back' or 'punched down', usually three-quarters of the way through the bulk fermentation period.

Knocking back is done for the following reasons:

+ to expel the gases and revitalise the yeast's activity
+ to even out the dough temperature; the outside of the dough will be colder than the inside
+ to stimulate and strengthen the gluten network
+ to even out the cell structure.

To knock back dough, gently push and fold it, using your hand. Once it has been knocked back, return dough to the container, cover and leave it until required for scaling.

Bulk fermentation and knocking back times are included, where relevant, in the recipes in this book.

THIS PAGE: The dough fully fermented in the bowl.
FACING PAGE: The fully fermented dough in the bowl as it is tipped out ready to be knocked back (image 1); dough being knocked back using the folding method (images 2–5); dough resting in glass bowl, covered in clingfilm (plastic wrap) for its final fermentation (image 6).

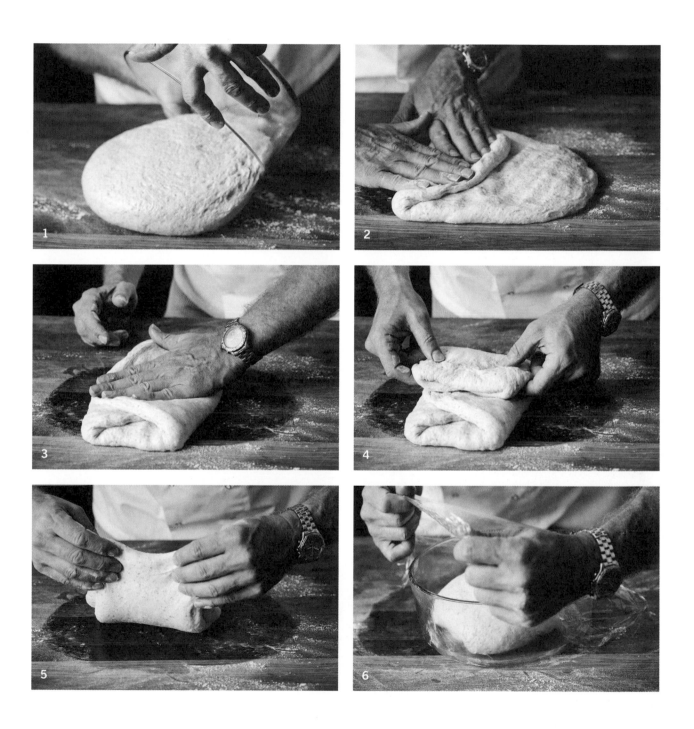

4. Dividing or scaling dough

The process of dividing – or scaling – dough takes place as soon as the dough has completed either its mixing or its bulk fermentation period. Using scales and a dough scraper, gently divide dough into the required sizes and weights. Do this as quickly as possible to avoid over-fermentation of the dough.

5. Rounding or pre-shaping dough

After the dough pieces have been scaled they are shaped into smooth, round balls. This helps to keep the gases within the fermenting dough rather than escaping into the air. To round or shape dough, place dough piece on a bare surface. Do not sprinkle flour on the surface, as you want the dough to grip the work surface. Cup your hand or hands over the dough piece. Applying gentle pressure, move the dough in a circular motion, making sure it is in contact with the work surface at all times. This movement stretches the surface of the dough so that it is completely smooth except for a seam at the bottom, where the dough has gripped the work surface.

6. Intermediate proof

Sometimes referred to as 'first proof', 'recovery time' or 'bench time', the intermediate proof is a resting period of 10–15 minutes between rounding or pre-shaping and final shaping that allows the gluten network to relax. If insufficient intermediate proof time is given, the dough will tear and become misshapen during final shaping. During the intermediate proof, cover dough pieces with clingfilm (plastic wrap), a dough cloth or a clean tea (dish) towel to keep the dough surface moist.

7. Final moulding and placing on trays

Once the dough piece has had its intermediate proof it is moulded into its final shape before being placed directly into loaf tins (pans), proofing baskets or onto baking trays (cookie sheets). Correct make-up or moulding is critical to the finished baked loaf or roll. All moulded bread doughs have a seam, and the seam should always be placed at the bottom on trays (sheets) and in tins (pans) (with the exception of cane proofing baskets or bannetons, where the smooth surface is placed at the bottom). Placing the loaf seam-side down avoids splitting during the baking process.

There are many different shapes that bread, rolls and buns can take: these are shown in different recipes in this book. Once the final shaping has taken place, toppings – e.g. sesame seeds, poppy seeds, cheese or flour – can be added before the final proof stage.

Dividing or scaling dough.

Rounding or pre-shaping dough.

Intermediate proof.

Moulding a round cob or boule loaf
Place dough on a lightly floured work surface. Fold all edges into the middle, then turn over so the scrunched side is on the work surface. Cup your hands over the risen dough and roll dough to form a tight ball. The dough should have a smooth surface, with the seam at the bottom.

Moulding a tin (pan) loaf
Flatten the risen dough into a rectangular shape (image 1), then roll into a tight pinwheel log (images 2–3). Place the dough seam-side down in the loaf tin/pan (images 4–5).

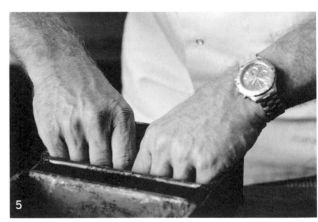

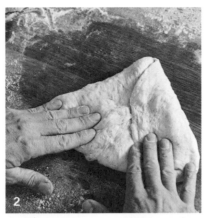

Moulding a baton loaf
Flatten the risen dough into a rectangular shape, then fold the top corners into the middle to meet each other, forming a 'bicycle seat' (images 1–2). Roll into a tight tapered log like a pinwheel (image 3). Seal the seam at the bottom (image 4) and then, using your hands at a tapered angle, roll to form a baton shape (with a thicker middle and thinner ends – see images 5–6). Place seam-side down on baking tray (cookie sheet).

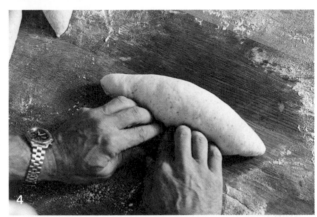

Moulding a baguette

Flatten the risen dough out to a long thin rectangle – this will take some time (image 1). You can also flick the dough up to stretch it (image 2). Place the rectangle on the work surface with the long edge facing you (image 3). Using your thumb and forefinger, roll the top edge over once (image 4), and use the heel of your hand to make a tight seal (images 5–7). Keep rolling and sealing all the way down to the bottom edge (image 8). This baguette shape should be nice and tight when you squeeze it. Place tightly moulded baguette on a floured, pleated couche cloth or tea (dish) towel and then pull the cloth up to keep the baguettes separate (images 9–10).

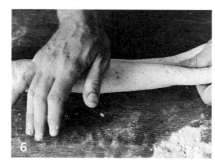

Moulding small round rolls

Divide the dough into small pieces for individual rolls (image 1), and place the dough pieces on a lightly floured surface. Fold all the edges of each dough piece into the middle (image 2). Turn the dough over so the scrunched side is on the work surface (image 3). Place your palm over the roll to form a cup and move your hand in a circular motion, feeling the ball of dough grip the work surface (image 4). Continue until the ball is round and has a smooth outer surface (image 5). Place seam-side down on a baking tray (cookie sheet).

8. Final proof

There are three main factors that need to be monitored closely throughout the final proofing stage.

1. Temperature: the dough should be left to prove in an area where the temperature is higher than the temperature of the dough. This prevents the dough from chilling and allows the yeast to function effectively. The ideal temperature for proving is between 35 and 40°C (95 and 104°F).

2. Humidity: use a spray bottle of water to keep the atmosphere humid while the dough is proving. Humidity is necessary at the final proving stage to prevent the dough from drying out and forming a skin. Dough that has formed a skin will not achieve a glossy crust during steaming and baking.

Lack of humidity will result in slow proving, and often a dry crust forms on the skin. Too much humidity will result in excessive heat (as humidity is produced by steam) and this could cause the dough to be parbaked.

3. Time: standard proof time can be anywhere between 45 and 90 minutes, depending on dough size, final dough temperature, yeast levels and ingredients used.

If you do not have a dough prover, loosely cover dough with a large sheet of clingfilm (plastic wrap) or a supermarket bag to retain the moisture, and set it in a warm, draught-free place such as the hot-water cupboard.

Cross-section of a fully proved loaf of bread. Notice the irregular gas bubbles, which will expand during baking and open up the texture of the bread to make it light and airy.

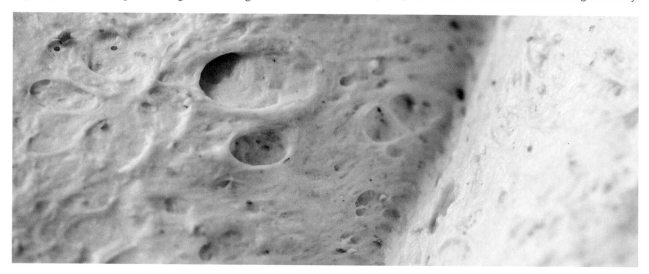

Testing dough for correct proof – the 'indentation test'

To test whether dough is fully proved to the correct size, use the 'indentation test'. Lightly press your finger into the side of the dough. If the indentation slowly springs back but does not go back to its original shape – instead it leaves a small indentation mark – the dough piece is ready to go in the oven.

Under-proved: if the indentation springs out quickly to its original shape, the dough is not fully proved. More proof time is required.

Correctly proved: when dough is lightly pressed, the indentation springs back but does not fully return to its original shape.

Over-proved: when lightly pressed, the dough piece will collapse and the indentation mark will not spring back. Preheat the oven immediately to the correct temperature and place dough piece directly into preheated oven. However, the product will be of poor quality.

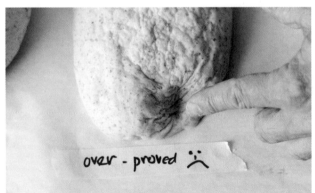

9. Decorating – cutting, seeding and dusting

There are various ways of decorating a loaf or bread rolls, including cutting, sprinkling the surface with seeds, or dusting with flour. Often a loaf will be cut and also dusted with flour to give a decorative pattern.

Cutting or slashing: cut slashes in the dough using a razor blade or a sharp knife. Always cut the dough when three-quarters proved, before it is fully proved: if using the indentation test, the dough will spring back at this stage.

Seeding: sprinkle seeds over the loaf or rolls to decorate. This may be done either after the final

shaping or just before the fully proved dough is put in the oven. If you are seeding the fully proved dough, lightly spray the loaf or rolls with water before sprinkling with seeds, so that the seeds adhere to the surface of the dough. Other toppings such as grated cheese, herbs or nuts may also be applied at this stage.

Dusting: dust the loaf or rolls with flour at full proof stage, before putting in the oven. The flour will bake onto the product.

Egg wash: brushing the loaf or rolls with egg wash before baking adds shine and colour.

10. Baking

This is the final and most important step in transforming the unpalatable, pale, wet dough into a light, porous, digestible and flavoursome product for consumption. Handle the dough with care when loading it into the preheated oven. This is important, because dough is fragile until the gluten has been 'set' by the baking process. The heat from the oven causes the yeast to lift the dough one more time before the yeast is killed by the heat. This is called oven spring.

Creating steam for crusty bread

For oven spring to happen, the oven must be hot and moist. This prevents the bread crust from drying out and being dull in colour. Steam gelatinises the starch in the dough and gives the loaf a glossy crust.

Professional bakers use a steam-injected oven. There are several ways to create steam in your domestic oven.

1. Spray the oven walls with warm water from a spray bottle.

2. Throw some ice cubes in a preheated baking dish at the bottom of the oven when you put the bread in to bake.

3. Place large rocks (not pebbles) in a roasting pan, then coil a metal chain around the rocks so it is evenly distributed among them. Place the pan of rocks and chain on the lowest rack in the oven at least 1–2 hours before putting the bread in the oven, to allow the rocks to fully heat up. When you load the bread into the oven, pull out the pan of hot rocks and chain and pour 250–375ml (1–1½ cups) of water over them (see page 27), then push it back in and immediately close the oven door. This produces an abundant amount of steam, which helps the bread to rise evenly, and the starch on the surface of the dough to gelatinise and begin to form a crust. If you want crusty bread, allow the steam to escape from the oven by leaving the door at least 5mm (¼in) ajar for at least 10 minutes before the end of baking. This gives the crust a chance to dry out.

Baking on a baking stone or pizza stone

Bread can be baked on a baking stone or pizza stone that has been preheated in the oven for 1 hour. To load the bread onto the preheated stone, place the proved dough on a baker's peel that has been well dusted with coarse semolina or cornmeal. Slide the peel into the oven, then with a quick forward and backward jerking movement, slide the dough piece onto the baking stone. Alternatively, place the dough on a tray lined with non-stick baking (parchment) paper and slide the loaf and the paper directly onto the preheated baking stone.

Baking on trays or in tins

Many bread products such as rolls, buns and loaves are baked on trays (sheets) or in tins (pans) that are placed directly onto the preheated baking stone or pizza stone.

Baking guidelines

Baking successful bread depends on time, temperature and dough weight.

Larger items are baked at higher temperatures and for longer – for example, 400–500g (14oz–1lb 2oz) dough pieces are baked at 220–230°C/425–446°F/Gas 7 for 30–40 minutes.

Smaller items require significantly less time and lower baking temperatures – for example, 100–200g (3½–7oz) dough pieces are baked at 200–210°C/400–410°F/Gas 6 for 15–18 minutes.

The longer the baking time:
  * the thicker the crust
  * the greater the moisture loss
  * the darker the crust.

The higher the baking temperature:
- the shorter the baking time
- the thinner the crust
- the more risk that larger dough pieces will be under-baked; items may collapse because the outside looks baked/dark and the inside is still under-baked. This is especially true with heavy-grain breads.

The lower the baking temperature:
- the longer the total baking time
- the thicker the crust
- the more the 'oven spring', as the yeast takes longer to kill off.

To tell whether a loaf of bread is correctly baked, tap the bottom of the loaf with your knuckles. If it sounds hollow, the loaf is correctly baked.

11. Cooling

After baking, bread must be left to cool; the flavour and aroma do not fully develop until the loaf has cooled completely. Always place baked breads directly onto a cooling rack or wire rack after baking, so the bottom of the bread does not sweat and become wet. Allow the bread to cool completely before slicing or cutting. This will ensure even slicing, and the texture will be shown to its full potential.

Storing

Breads that are to be served within 8 hours may be left in the open air or in a paper bag. Do not package crusty bread, as the crust will soften and become leathery. If storing bread in the freezer, place it in a plastic bag to extend its shelf life. Never place bread in the refrigerator, as this speeds up the staling process.

Sourdough

Sourdough (also known as levain, lievito naturale, poolish, etc.) is a natural yeast developed from wild yeasts and lactic acid bacteria. The exact origins of sourdough are unknown, but historical sources show that it was used in bread preparation in Egypt around 4000 BC. The Greeks kneaded flour with grape juice to make special bread for celebrations. The Gauls used fermented barley to make sourdough, and this practice spread throughout Europe. In the fifteenth century, beer yeast (barm) was used instead of sourdough.

It is likely that initially the dough turned sour by mistake, and to correct this, it was kneaded again with more flour. After some time the dough achieved a spongy structure, and the resultant bread was tastier and softer. This accidental discovery may have been the starting point for the development of sourdough. According to Italian tradition, sourdough was passed from family to family for the preparation of the weekly bread, a tradition kept till recent times.

In the nineteenth century, Louis Pasteur's experiments with microorganisms led to the use of cultured yeasts, which replaced sourdough.

Today sourdough is not extensively used, for several reasons. The process involves many time-consuming steps, and is quite complex and inflexible. Shorter processes are more economical; however, these do not give the unique results of a sourdough starter.

Natural yeast

Sourdough (levain) is a natural yeast produced through the fermentation of flour and water and developed by wild yeast and lactic bacteria, without the addition of any compressed yeast. The fermentation process is complex, inflexible, long and labour-intensive because of the different multiplication steps needed.

Any flour dough that is left to rest for a prolonged time will start to ferment. The process is started by the microorganisms present in the air and in the flour; or by inoculation with fermented fruit; or by using a starter culture. The fermentation process is controlled by adjusting the conditions, including temperature, time and dough consistency.

Important facts on sourdough:

+ The dough triples in volume in 4 hours.
+ The dough has a thin skin.

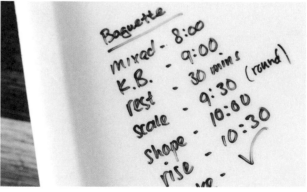

- The taste is sour-sweet and well rounded.
- The dough is not sticky.
- The dough has a high level of acidity, with pH level between 3.95 and 4.05.
- Fermentation is a long, non-flexible process.
- There is slow release of carbon dioxide gas, resulting in an irrregular and non-uniform crumb.
- The dough has better colour, friability and softness.
- Sourdough bread has a longer shelf life.

Enzymes

Enzymes are biological catalysts that are essential for governing the fermentation process. The biological reactions would proceed at a very slow rate or would require more drastic conditions to reach a speed equivalent to those observed during fast fermentation.

All enzymes are proteins naturally designed to work effectively under mild conditions, within narrow bands of temperature and acidity and with a highly specific action – each enzyme acts only on a single substrate. In some cases the raw material may not contain sufficient enzymes to catalyse the fermentation, in which case it is useful to add some, for example vitamin C or enzyme-active malt flour.

Bacteria

Flour always contains lactic acid bacteria and acetic acid bacteria, which contribute to the fermentation process, converting sugar into lactic and acetic acid. Lactic acid bacteria ferment glucose to lactic acid. Acetic acid bacteria convert the alcohol produced by yeast into acetic acid. Both kinds of bacteria contribute to build up good gluten characteristics and produce acidification, which inhibits the growth of spoiling organisms.

The ratio of lactic acid to acetic acid should be 3 to 1, in order to achieve a uniform elasticity of gluten. Lactic acid gives a more elastic gluten network, while acetic acid gives a more rigid structure. This ratio also exerts a strong influence in achieving the typical and unique flavour characteristics of sourdough and contributes to retarding the staling, one of the most serious problems of leavened products.

Warm fermentation increases lactic acid fermentation, while cool and firm dough reduces lactic acid and gives almost the same amount of acetic acid.

Refer to the Basic Recipe section (page 186) for sourdough levain recipes.

Savoury Breads & Sourdoughs

Petites Baguettes Traditionnelles

In this hybrid dough I use levain or natural wild yeast combined with commercial dry yeast – the levain for the complex flavour, and dry yeast for lightness in crumb. Remember to only three-quarters prove the baguettes before scoring them and placing them in the oven: this will create that characteristic bursting cut that French baguettes are known for.

MAKES 8 SMALL BAGUETTES

480g (3 cups) strong bread flour

20g (2¾ tbsp) wholemeal or whole wheat flour

10g (2 tsp) salt

5g (1½ tsp) malt flour (enzyme-active malt flour is best)

3g (1 tsp) instant dry yeast

100g (3½oz) Sourdough Levain Starter (page 186)

360–370ml (scant 1½ cups) chilled water

additional flour for dusting

Place all dry ingredients and the starter in a large mixing bowl. Add the water and, using a wooden spoon, combine to form a dough. Tip dough out onto a lightly floured surface and knead for 10–15 minutes, resting it for 30 seconds every 2–3 minutes, until it feels smooth and elastic. Place dough in a lightly oiled large bowl, cover with clingfilm (plastic wrap) and leave in a warm place for 1 hour, until almost doubled in size.

Tip dough onto a floured work surface and gently deflate by folding it onto itself three or four times, then return it to the bowl, cover with clingfilm (plastic wrap) and leave for a further 30 minutes in a warm place.

Gently tip dough onto a lightly floured work surface and divide into eight equal pieces, approximately 120g (4oz) each. Flatten each piece of dough into a small rectangle and roll up into a tight Swiss (jelly) roll (see page 38). Roll each piece out to a small baguette shape, 15–18cm (6–7in) in length, with tapered ends. Roll each baguette in flour and place seam-side down on a tea (dish) towel that has been dusted with flour. Make a pleat in the tea (dish) towel between each baguette to keep them separate. Cover with clingfilm (plastic wrap) and leave to prove for approximately 15 minutes. The dough should be still slightly active to the touch, almost a little under-proved (it will spring back when you touch it with your finger). Do not over-prove (rise).

Line two baking trays (cookie sheets) with baking (parchment) paper. Gently lift each baguette and place on prepared baking trays (cookie sheets). Lightly dust baguettes with flour if you like. Using a sharp knife or a razor blade, make three diagonal slashes across the top of each baguette; the blade should be at a 45° angle, and the cut should be a shallow incision rather than a deep cut.

Place trays in a preheated 240°C/475°F/Gas 9 oven, apply steam (page 44) and close oven door quickly. Bake for 15 minutes. Rotate trays, reduce oven temperature to 200°C/400°F/Gas 6 and bake for a further 10 minutes or until baguettes are dark golden brown and the bottoms sound hollow when tapped. Place on a wire rack to cool.

Fill baguettes with your favourite sandwich fillings.

Turkish Pide

What's not to like about this versatile bread with its characteristic super-soft crust, topped with black sesame seeds or nigella seeds? You can use it as a sandwich bread, to accompany a curry, or serve it as a starter with a fine olive oil, dukkah and aged balsamic vinegar. I often sneak 5 grams of cumin seed into the dough during the mixing stage – wonderful!

MAKES 3 LARGE OR 6 SMALL PIDE

500g (3 cups) strong bread flour
10g (2 tsp) salt
20ml (4 tsp) olive oil
10g (2 heaping tsp) sugar
5g (1¼ tsp) instant dry yeast
380ml (1½ cups) water

1 egg whisked with 50ml (scant ¼ cup) water, for egg wash
100g (¾ cup) black sesame seeds or nigella seeds
additional flour for dusting

Place all ingredients except egg wash and seeds in a large mixing bowl. Using a wooden spoon, combine ingredients to form a dough. Tip dough out onto a lightly floured work surface and knead for 10–15 minutes, resting for 30 seconds every 2–3 minutes, until dough is smooth and elastic. The dough will be sticky to the touch at first. It's okay to add a little extra flour during the kneading process, but don't be tempted to add excessive amounts as it will result in a dry loaf.

Lightly oil a large bowl with olive oil. Place dough in bowl and cover with clingfilm (plastic wrap). Allow to rise in a warm place for 1½ hours, until dough has doubled in size. Turn dough out onto a floured surface and cut into 3 x 300g (11oz) pieces (for large pides) or 6 x 150g (5oz) pieces (for small pides). Very gently and loosely mould the dough pieces into oblong shapes, being careful not to knock too much gas out of the dough. Cover with clingfilm (plastic wrap) and leave to rest on the floured work surface for 20 minutes.

Line a baking tray (cookie sheet) with baking (parchment) paper. Using your hands and fingers, coax and stretch the dough pieces gently into an oblong shape. Place on baking tray (cookie sheet), leaving a gap of 3–4cm (1¼–1½in) between each loaf. Using a pastry brush, brush with egg wash. Using floured fingers, make a series of indentations down the length of each loaf. Lightly sprinkle with black sesame seeds or nigella seeds and set aside for another 20 minutes to rise.

Place loaves in a preheated 250°C/500°F/Gas 10 oven. Bake for 9–10 minutes until lightly baked, with brown and white spots all over. Remove from oven and place on a wire rack to cool.

Pain aux Noix en Couronne (Walnut Crown Bread)

I couldn't write a bread book without including walnut bread! This loaf is packed full of walnuts and goes wonderfully on a cheeseboard. Use the freshest walnuts you can find. Leftover bread can be sliced finely and toasted dry to use as walnut crisps.

MAKES 2 LOAVES

400g (scant 2½ cups) strong bread flour

100g (1 cup) rye flour

100g (3½oz) Sourdough Levain Starter (page 186) – must be healthy, live and fed at least 8 hours before using

5g (1½ tsp) malt flour (enzyme-active malt flour is best)

30g (1½ tbsp) honey

10g (2 heaping tsp) salt

5g (1¼ tsp) instant dry yeast

320ml (1¼ cups) (approx.) chilled water

275g (2¾ cups) walnuts, lightly toasted and roughly chopped

additional flour for dusting

Place all ingredients except walnuts in a large mixing bowl and, using a wooden spoon, combine to form a dough. Tip dough out onto a lightly floured surface and knead for around 15 minutes, resting it for 1 minute every 2–3 minutes, until dough is smooth and elastic. Add the walnuts and very gently incorporate into the dough, taking your time and being careful not to smash the walnut pieces. When well combined, place dough in a lightly oiled bowl, cover with clingfilm (plastic wrap) and leave in a warm place for 1 hour, until doubled in bulk.

Tip dough onto work surface and gently deflate by folding it onto itself three or four times. Return it to the bowl, cover with clingfilm (plastic wrap) and leave in a warm place for a further 30 minutes, until dough is gassy and bubbly.

Gently tip dough onto a lightly floured work surface, divide it into two pieces, approximately 600g (1¼lb) each, and very gently and loosely shape each piece into a round ball. Cover with clingfilm (plastic wrap) and leave to rest for 20 minutes. Line two baking trays (cookie sheets) with baking (parchment) paper.

Flatten out a dough piece, then tightly roll it up towards you like a pinwheel, applying pressure with your hands as you roll – the tighter the better. Keep rolling it until it is approximately 60cm (23in) long. Roll it in flour to coat, then shape into a ring with a good-sized hole in the centre. Place on prepared baking tray (cookie sheet). Repeat with second dough piece. Dust dough rings with more flour, if needed. Cover loaves with clingfilm (plastic wrap) and leave to prove for approximately 45 minutes, until three-quarters proved (use indentation test, page 41). Using a razor blade or a sharp knife, cut four slashes on the top of each ring after dough has proved and just before it goes into the oven.

Place loaves on trays (sheets) into a preheated 240°C/475°F/Gas 9 oven, apply steam (see page 44) then quickly close the oven door. Bake for 20 minutes, then swap trays (sheets) around to ensure an even bake, reduce oven temperature to 200°C/400°F/Gas 6 and bake for a further 15–20 minutes, until loaves are a dark golden brown and the bottom sounds hollow when tapped. Place on a wire rack to cool.

Beetroot & Thyme Baguettes

The strong, earthy taste of beetroot goes perfectly with thyme to create this baguette. The starter dough adds natural fermented flavour.

MAKES 6 BAGUETTES

STARTER DOUGH
200g (scant 1¼ cups) strong bread flour

3g (1 tsp) instant dry yeast

2 tbsp fresh thyme, finely chopped

150ml (⅔ cup) cold water

DOUGH
500g (3 cups) strong bread flour

15g (1 tbsp) salt

5g (1 tsp) sugar

5g (1¼ tsp) instant dry yeast

1 quantity of Starter Dough

250g (9oz) raw beetroot, peeled and coarsely grated

250ml (1 cup) chilled water

additional flour for dusting

Make the starter dough in advance. Place all ingredients in a medium mixing bowl and mix together until a smooth, soft dough is formed. Scrape down the sides of the bowl and leave dough to double in size (4 hours at room temperature, or overnight in the refrigerator).

Place all dough ingredients except water in a large mixing bowl. Add water and, using a wooden spoon, combine to form a dough. Tip out onto a lightly floured surface and knead for 10–15 minutes, resting it for 30 seconds every 2–3 minutes, until dough is smooth and elastic.

Lightly oil a large bowl. Place dough in bowl, cover with clingfilm (plastic wrap) and leave in a warm place for 1 hour, until almost doubled in size. Tip dough onto the work surface and gently deflate by folding it back onto itself three or four times. Return dough to bowl, cover with clingfilm (plastic wrap) and leave a further 30 minutes in a warm place.

Gently tip dough onto a lightly floured work surface and divide into six equal pieces approximately 215g (7½oz) each. Flatten each piece of dough into a small rectangle and roll up into a tight Swiss (jelly) roll (see page 38). Continue to roll into small baguette shapes, 25–30cm (10–12in) length, with tapered ends.

Line two baking trays (cookie sheets) with baking (parchment) paper. Roll baguettes in flour, then place them on the prepared trays (sheets). Cover with clingfilm (plastic wrap) and leave to prove for 20–30 minutes. The dough should still be a little under-proved – it should be active and alive when pressed with your finger.

Using a razor blade or a sharp knife, make 4–5 diagonal slashes across the top of each baguette. The blade should be at a 45° angle, and the cut should be a shallow incision rather than a deep cut.

Place baking trays (cookie sheets) in a preheated 240–250°C/475–500°F/Gas 9–10 oven, apply steam (page 44) and close oven door quickly. Bake for 18 minutes, then reduce oven temperature to 200°C/400°F/Gas 6 and swap top and bottom trays (sheets) for an even bake. Bake for a further 8–10 minutes until baguettes are crisp, dark golden brown in colour, and the bottom sounds hollow when tapped. Remove from oven and place on a wire rack to cool.

Dean's Sourdough (Pain au Levain)

This is one of my signature breads in all of my bakeries. It's a full-on 100 per cent sourdough made with natural wild yeast. You can vary the amounts of plain (all-purpose), rye and wholemeal (whole wheat) flour to create your own special loaf. This recipe makes two loaves. You can bake the two loaves at different times, if you wish – just bring the first loaf out of the refrigerator 1 hour before the second loaf, so there is a gap between baking. Remember to slash the loaves when they are three-quarters proved (risen), before baking – this will create a nice burst during baking.

MAKES 2 SOURDOUGH LOAVES

680g (generous 4 cups) strong bread flour

80g (½ cup) wholemeal or whole wheat flour

40g (¼ cup) rye flour

360g (12oz) Sourdough Levain Starter (page 186) – healthy, live and fed at least 8 hours before using

8g (2 heaping tsp) malt flour (enzyme-active malt flour is best)

20g (1 heaping tbsp) salt

520ml (2 cups) (approx.) chilled water

additional flour for dusting

Place all ingredients in a large mixing bowl. Using a wooden spoon, combine ingredients to form a dough. Tip dough out onto a lightly floured work surface and knead for around 15 minutes, resting for 1 minute every 2–3 minutes, until dough is smooth and elastic. Place dough in a lightly oiled bowl, cover with clingfilm (plastic wrap) and leave in a warm place for about 3 hours until almost doubled in size.

Tip dough onto a floured work surface. Gently deflate dough by folding it back onto itself three or four times. Return dough to bowl, cover with clingfilm (plastic wrap) and leave a further 1 hour in a warm place. The dough should be really gassy and bubbly by now, full of life and energy.

Gently tip dough onto a lightly floured work surface. Divide into two pieces, approximately 820g (1¾lb) each. Very gently and loosely, mould each piece into a round ball shape. Cover and rest for 15 minutes.

While the dough is resting, lay a tea (dish) towel inside a round cane basket or medium round bowl and heavily dust the tea (dish) towel with flour to create an even layer that the dough will rest on during its final proof; or, if you have a banneton, dust it heavily with flour.

Mould each dough piece into a round ball shape, making sure the ball is tight and firm. Gently place dough balls into the flour-dusted basket or banneton, with smooth-side down and seam-side up. Dust with flour. Cover with clingfilm (plastic wrap). Leave in a warm place for approximately 45 minutes, then place in the refrigerator overnight (12–14 hours). This will develop the flavour and texture of the loaf.

Remove dough in baskets from the refrigerator and leave to rise at room temperature for 2–2½ hours, making sure dough is still covered with clingfilm (plastic wrap).

Recipe continued overleaf

Place one dough piece back in the refrigerator while you bake the first loaf. Line a baking tray (cookie sheet) or a baker's peel with baking (parchment) paper. Gently tip the dough ball onto the baking (parchment) paper. Using a razor blade or sharp knife, make four cuts in the top surface.

Slide loaf and baking (parchment) paper onto a hot baking tray (cookie sheet) or baking stone in a preheated 250°C/500°F/Gas 10 oven. Apply steam to the oven (page 44) and quickly close oven door. Bake for 20 minutes, then rotate loaf, reduce oven temperature to 200°C/400°F/Gas 6 and bake for a further 15–20 minutes or until dark golden brown and the bottom sounds hollow when tapped. Remove from oven and place on a wire rack to cool.

Suggested time guide for making Pain au Levain	
8.00am	final feed of levain starter
2.30pm	weigh dough ingredients
2.40pm	begin to mix and knead dough
3.00pm	place dough in oiled bowl, cover and ferment for 3 hours
6.00pm	gently knock back dough, return to bowl, cover and rest
7.00pm	divide dough into two, shape into a loose round shape (for the intermediate proof), place on floured work surface, cover and rest for 15 minutes
7.15pm	shape dough pieces into their final shape and place in floured cloth-lined bowl (banneton), cover and rise for 45 minutes
8.00pm	lightly dust top of dough with flour, cover and place in refrigerator overnight (approximately 12 hours)
Next day	
8.00am	remove dough from refrigerator and rise at room temperature for 2–2½ hours
9.15am	preheat oven with baking stone in place
10.00am (approx.)	bake Pain au Levain
10.40am (approx.)	remove from oven and cool on wire rack

Farmhouse White Loaf

Sometimes it's nice to have a simple basic loaf of white bread. Here is that recipe. This loaf is not meant to last five days, like some store-bought packaged bread full of enzymes, emulsifiers and E numbers. It contains six basic ingredients to produce a fantastic loaf of bread that will disappear fast once you cut the first slice.

MAKES 2 LOAVES

500g (3 cups) strong bread flour
10g (2 tsp) salt
10g (2 heaping tsp) sugar
7g (2½ tsp) instant dry yeast
20ml (4 tsp) olive oil
370ml (1½ cups) water
additional flour for dusting

Place all ingredients in a large mixing bowl. Using a wooden spoon, combine to form a dough. Tip dough out onto a lightly floured surface and knead for 15–20 minutes, resting for 1 minute every 2–3 minutes, until dough feels smooth and elastic. The dough will be sticky to the touch at first. Adding a little extra flour while kneading is okay, but don't be tempted to add excessive amounts of flour during the kneading process.

Lightly oil a bowl large enough to allow dough to double in bulk. Put dough into bowl and cover with clingfilm (plastic wrap). Leave in a warmish place (23–25°C/73–77°F) for 1 hour. Knock back dough in bowl by gently folding it back onto itself. This will deflate the dough slightly, but it will develop more strength. Cover with clingfilm (plastic wrap) and leave for 30 minutes.

Tip dough out onto a lightly floured work surface. Divide dough into two equal pieces, and gently shape each piece into a roundish shape. Cover with clingfilm (plastic wrap) and leave to rest for 15 minutes (intermediate proof).

Grease two 500g (1 lb/2 oz) loaf tins (pans). Remove clingfilm (plastic wrap) from dough. Flatten and mould dough pieces into a rectangular loaf shape (page 36). Place into loaf tins (pans). Alternatively, cut each dough piece into two equal pieces. Mould each piece into a round cob shape (page 35) and place two cobs side by side in each tin (pan). Cover loaves with clingfilm (plastic wrap) and leave to prove for 1 hour.

Remove clingfilm (plastic wrap) and dust loaves with flour (using a sieve), if desired. Using a sharp knife or razor blade, cut straight down the centre of each loaf lengthways, approximately 5mm (¼in) deep.

Place loaves in a preheated 230°C/450°F/Gas 8 oven. Apply steam (page 44), then quickly close the oven door. Bake loaves for 30–35 minutes or until the bottom of the loaf sounds hollow when tapped with your knuckles. Remove from oven and place on a wire rack to cool.

Olive & Oven-roasted Tomato Panini

Every time I go to the famed Italian Princi Bakery in Wardour Street in London, I buy one of these and enjoy it with a glass of Riesling and just sit there watching the world go by. I have added a little fresh thyme to the dough to make it mine – but inspired by Princi. Make sure the olives are whole or, at the very least, a combination of whole and some cut lengthways.

MAKES APPROXIMATELY 10 PANINI

30 cherry tomatoes
salt and pepper

DOUGH
500g (3 cups) strong bread flour
100g (3½oz) Sourdough Levain
Starter (see page 186)
10g (2 tsp) salt
5g (1¼ tsp) instant dry yeast
1 tbsp fresh thyme leaves
350ml (1½ cups) water

350g (2 cups) whole black or
green olives, pitted
additional flour for dusting

Line a baking tray (cookie sheet) with baking (parchment) paper. Cut cherry tomatoes in half, place on prepared baking tray (cookie sheet) and sprinkle each half with a pinch of salt and pepper. Bake in a preheated 150°C/300°F/Gas 2 oven for 10 minutes, taking care not to let them get too soft. Set aside to cool.

Place all dough ingredients except the water in a large mixing bowl. Add water and, using a wooden spoon, combine to form a dough.

Tip dough out onto the work surface and knead for 10–15 minutes, resting it for 30 seconds every 2–3 minutes, until dough is smooth and elastic. Add olives and knead in gently until they are evenly distributed throughout the dough. Place dough in a lightly oiled large bowl, cover with clingfilm (plastic wrap) and leave in a warm place for 1 hour, until almost doubled in size.

Tip dough onto the work surface and gently deflate by folding it onto itself three or four times, then return it to the bowl, cover with clingfilm (plastic wrap) and leave in a warm place for a further 30 minutes. Line two baking trays (cookie sheets) with baking (parchment) paper.

Gently tip dough onto a well-floured work surface and divide into 10 equal pieces. Using plenty of flour, very gently fold each piece into a flattish rectangle, then stud the surface of each with five or six tomato halves. Place panini on prepared baking trays (cookie sheets), cover with clingfilm (plastic wrap) and leave to rise for 30 minutes.

Place baking trays (cookie sheets) in a preheated 240°C/475°F/Gas 9 oven, apply steam (see page 44) and quickly close oven door. Bake for 20–25 minutes, until golden brown.

Polenta Petites Boules

These are pretty as a button, and great for a dinner party. The cooked polenta (cornmeal) gives a lovely colour and moistness to the crumb, and the brown sugar adds a rich, deep-brown, caramelised crust. Prepare the polenta a day in advance. Reheat these rolls in the oven at 180°C/350°F/Gas 4 for 10 minutes before serving with a good-quality smoked salted butter.

MAKES 12 ROLLS

POLENTA
30g (3½ tbsp) coarse polenta or cornmeal
170ml (¾ cup) water

DOUGH
500g (3 cups) strong bread flour
10g (2 tsp) salt
40g (scant ¼ cup packed) brown sugar
5g (1¼ tsp) instant dry yeast
1 quantity of cooked Polenta (from the day before)
260ml (1 cup) milk

additional flour for dusting

Prepare the polenta a day in advance. Place polenta and water into a saucepan and bring to the boil, turn heat to low and cook for 2 minutes, stirring all the time. Pour into a bowl, cover and leave to cool, preferably overnight.

The next day, place all ingredients in a large mixing bowl and, using a wooden spoon, combine to form a dough.

Tip dough out onto a lightly floured surface and knead for 15 minutes, resting it for 1 minute every 2–3 minutes, until dough is smooth and elastic. Check dough while kneading for stickiness: add a little more water or flour if necessary to achieve a soft, but not too firm dough. Place dough in a lightly oiled bowl, cover with clingfilm (plastic wrap) and leave in a warm place for approximately 1½ hours, until dough has doubled in size.

Gently knock back dough in the bowl by folding it back onto itself several times, then cover again and leave for a further 30–45 minutes until almost doubled in size. Line a baking tray (cookie sheet) with baking (parchment) paper.

Tip dough onto a lightly floured work surface, divide into 12 equal pieces, approximately 80g (3oz) each, and roll each piece into a small ball or bun shape (page 39). Roll dough balls in flour to coat, then place seam-side down on prepared baking tray, leaving a 2–3cm (¾–1¼in) gap between each roll. Cover with clingfilm (plastic wrap) and leave to prove (rise) for 45–60 minutes, until they are nice and bold in shape, but not flat and wrinkly (over-proved).

Dust rolls again with flour and, using a razor blade or a sharp knife, make a trellis pattern of little decorative cuts in the surface of the rolls that will expand during baking. Place baking tray (cookie sheet) in a preheated 230°C/450°F/Gas 8 oven, apply steam (see page 44) and quickly close the oven door. Bake for 18–20 minutes, turning the baking tray (cookie sheet) around halfway through to ensure even cooking. Remove from oven and place on a wire rack to cool.

Black Onion-seed Bagels

These savoury bagels are great served with smoked salmon, red onion rings, capers and cream cheese. They also go perfectly with scrambled eggs and salmon or grilled (broiled) bacon.

MAKES 10 BAGELS

DOUGH

500g (3 cups) strong bread flour
10g (2 tsp) salt
15g (1 tbsp) soft brown sugar
15ml (1 tbsp) olive oil
5g (1¼ tsp) instant dry yeast
50g (⅓ cup) onion, very finely chopped
40g (2 tbsp) black onion seeds
270ml (1 cup) chilled water (place in refrigerator overnight)

200g (1¼ cups) coarse semolina or polenta (cornmeal), to lay bagels on
2 tbsp liquid honey
50g (5 tbsp) black onion seeds, to decorate

Line a baking tray (cookie sheet) with baking (parchment) paper and sprinkle liberally with coarse semolina or polenta (cornmeal). Place all dough ingredients in a large mixing bowl. Using your hands, combine ingredients to form a dough. The dough will be very firm, but don't be tempted to add any water or your bagels will go out of shape when you boil them. Tip the dough out onto a lightly floured surface and knead for 10–15 minutes, resting it for 30 seconds every 2–3 minutes, until dough is smooth and elastic.

Immediately cut dough into 10 strips approximately 90g (3¼oz) each. Roll each strip into a rope approximately 15cm (6in) long. Wrap a dough rope around all four fingers of one hand, with the two ends meeting together underneath your fingers (see image 1). Apply pressure on the work surface as you roll to seal the ends together into a ring shape (see image 2). Once the bagels are formed, place on the prepared baking tray (cookie sheet), leaving a 2cm (¾in) gap between bagels. Cover loosely with clingfilm (plastic wrap) and place tray (sheet) in the refrigerator overnight, for 12–16 hours.

Remove bagels from refrigerator and leave to stand at room temperature for 30–45 minutes. Line a baking tray (cookie sheet) with baking (parchment) paper.

Fill a large saucepan with water, add the honey and bring to the boil over a high heat. With water at full boil, place two or three bagels into the saucepan and blanch for 30 seconds on each side, a total of 1 minute (see image 3). Using a slotted spoon, gently remove bagels from the boiling water, making sure all the water has drained off. Place bagels semolina-side down onto the lined baking tray (cookie sheet), leaving a 2cm (¾in) space between each bagel. Immediately sprinkle with black onion seeds while surface is still wet.

Bake in a preheated 220°C/425°F/Gas 7 oven for 20–25 minutes or until a shiny golden brown. Remove bagels from oven, place on a wire rack and leave to cool completely.

Two-olive Baton

There is nothing more satisfying than a good loaf of bread chock-full of olives. The secret is not to chop the olives too small – you want large pieces throughout the loaf. I have combined a little sourdough levain starter to give it a slightly acidic flavour.

MAKES 3 BATONS

500g (3 cups) strong bread flour

100g (3½oz) Sourdough Levain Starter (page 186)

10g (2 tsp) salt

10ml (2 tsp) olive oil

5g (1¼ tsp) instant dry yeast

310ml (1¼ cups) water

150g (scant 1 cup) green olives, pitted and roughly chopped

150g (scant 1 cup) kalamata or black olives, pitted and roughly chopped

semolina flour for dusting (or use plain/all-purpose flour)

In a large bowl place flour, levain starter, salt, olive oil and yeast. Mix to combine. Add water and, using a wooden spoon, combine to form a dough.

Tip dough out onto a lightly floured work surface and knead for 10–15 minutes, resting it for 30 seconds every 2–3 minutes, until dough is smooth and elastic. Add chopped olives and very gently knead to evenly incorporate them into the dough, taking care not to mash them too much. This takes time – don't be tempted to rush this stage.

Place dough in a lightly oiled large bowl, cover with clingfilm (plastic wrap) and leave in a warm place for about 1 hour, until almost doubled. Tip dough onto the work surface and gently deflate it by folding onto itself three or four times. Return it to the bowl, cover with clingfilm (plastic wrap) and leave in a warm place for a further 30 minutes.

Tip dough onto a lightly floured work surface and divide into three equal pieces. Flatten each piece into a small rectangle and roll up tightly like a Swiss (jelly) roll, with tapered ends (see page 37). Roll shaped dough in flour and place seam-side up in a tea (dish) towel that has been dusted with flour. Separate the dough pieces by pulling part of the tea (dish) towel between each one. Cover with clingfilm (plastic wrap) and leave to prove for 30–45 minutes; the dough should be still slightly active to the touch, almost a little under-proved.

Line two baking trays (cookie sheets) with baking (parchment) paper. Gently lift each dough piece and place seam-side down on the prepared trays (sheets). Dust lightly with semolina flour and, using a sharp knife or razor blade, make three diagonal slashes across the top of each dough piece. Place trays (sheets) in a preheated 240°C/475°F/Gas 9 oven, add steam (page 44) then close oven door quickly. Bake for 15 minutes, then turn trays (sheets) around, reduce oven temperature to 200°C/400°F/Gas 6 and bake for a further 20 minutes or until batons are a dark golden brown and the bottoms sound hollow when tapped. Remove from oven and place on a wire rack to cool.

Onion Fougasse

A fougasse is a flat bread that is great to have when friends are over – it is designed to be ripped apart and shared. Dip chunks of fougasse into a hearty winter soup, olive oil, or a good hummus or savoury dip. Explore different savoury fillings for fougasse, such as olives, sundried tomatoes, mixed herbs, chilli, diced apple and cheese.

MAKES 4 LOAVES

FERMENTED DOUGH
60g (⅓ cup) strong bread flour
pinch of salt
1g (½ tsp) instant dry yeast
40ml (8 tsp) water

DOUGH
400g (scant 2½ cups) strong bread flour
1 quantity of Fermented Dough (from the day before)
8g (1 heaping tsp) salt
7g (2½ tsp) instant dry yeast
10ml (2 tsp) olive oil
260ml (1 cup) water
120g (4oz) red onion, finely sliced

additional flour for dusting

Make the fermented dough a day in advance. Mix all the ingredients in a mixing bowl to form a dough. Tip dough onto a well-floured work surface and knead until fully developed. This should take 8–10 minutes. Place dough in a lightly oiled container. Cover with clingfilm (plastic wrap) and leave overnight to ferment, at least 12–16 hours.

To make dough, place all ingredients except the onion in a large mixing bowl. Using a wooden spoon, combine the ingredients to form a dough. Tip dough out onto a lightly floured surface and knead for 10–15 minutes, resting it for 1 minute every 2–3 minutes, until it feels smooth and elastic. Add onion and continue to knead. It will take a while for the onion to become fully incorporated into the dough; however, take your time. The dough will appear sticky at first, but this will disappear with time. You can add a sprinkling of flour during this stage, but don't add too much as it will stiffen the dough and make the fougasse dry.

Lightly oil a bowl large enough for dough to double in bulk. Put dough in bowl and cover with clingfilm (plastic wrap). Leave in a warmish place (23–25°C/73–77°F) for 1 hour. Gently knock back the dough in the bowl by folding it back onto itself. This will deflate it slightly, but it will develop more strength. Cover again with clingfilm (plastic wrap) and leave for 30 minutes.

Tip dough out onto a lightly floured work surface. Using a dough scraper, cut dough into four pieces approximately 250g (9oz) each. Gently and loosely mould each dough piece into a tear shape. Lay the pieces back on the floured work surface, cover with clingfilm (plastic wrap) and leave to rest for 15 minutes.

Using the palm of your hand, flatten each dough piece on the floured work surface, keeping the tear shape, to approximately 150mm x 100mm x 10mm (6in x 4in x ½in) thick. Using a sharp knife or dough scraper, make three diagonal cuts down each side of the tear shape, and two lengthways down the middle, each cut approximately 50mm (2in) in length and all the way through the dough. Pull each cut wide apart to give a leaf-shaped loaf with large, open gashes in it. Repeat for the remaining dough pieces.

Line two baking trays (cookie sheets) with baking (parchment) paper. Place each dough piece onto the baking paper, two per baking tray, keeping the cuts wide open and apart. Allow about 50mm (2in) between each dough piece. Cover baking trays with clingfilm (plastic wrap) and leave in a warm place to prove for 15 minutes.

Place baking trays in a preheated 240–250°C/475–500°F/Gas 9–10 oven, apply steam (page 44) and close oven door quickly. Bake for 18 minutes, then reduce oven temperature to 200°C/400°F/Gas 6, rotate trays, and bake for a further 8–10 minutes, until fougasses are well baked, crisp and not pale. Remove from oven and turn out onto a wire rack to cool.

VARIATION: Substitute sliced pitted olives for the onion; take care not to mix the olives in too strongly as they will crush and stain the dough black.

Cheese, Bacon & Onion Pavés

These little savoury loaves shaped like paving stones (pavés) are full of flavour and easy to make. Put some in your lunchbox, or eat them as a snack with a cold beer.

MAKES 6–8 PAVÉS

500g (3 cups) strong bread flour
10g (2 tsp) salt
20ml (4 tsp) olive oil
5g (1 tsp) sugar
7g (2½ tsp) instant dry yeast
350ml (1½ cups) water

FILLING
300g (3 cups) grated strong Cheddar or tasty cheese
1 medium onion, sliced in rings
6 rashers (slices) smoky bacon

additional flour for dusting
100g (1 cup) extra grated Cheddar, for topping

Place flour, salt, oil, sugar and yeast in a large mixing bowl. Add water and, using a wooden spoon, combine the ingredients to form a dough. Tip dough out onto a lightly floured surface and knead for 10–15 minutes, resting for 1 minute every 2–3 minutes, until dough is smooth and elastic.

Place dough in a lightly oiled large bowl, cover with clingfilm (plastic wrap) and leave in a warm place for 1 hour until almost doubled in size. Tip dough onto work surface and gently deflate by folding it back onto itself three or four times. Return it to the bowl, cover with clingfilm (plastic wrap) and leave in a warm place for a further 30 minutes.

Line a baking tray (cookie sheet) with baking (parchment) paper. Gently tip dough onto a lightly floured work surface and, using a rolling pin, roll out to a 75cm x 15cm (29in x 6in) rectangle. Position the dough rectangle on the work surface with the long edge facing you. Sprinkle dough evenly with grated cheese, onion and strips of bacon. Fold top edge of dough slightly more than halfway down over the filling. Using a pastry brush dipped in water, brush the folded dough surface. Then fold the bottom dough edge with its filling upwards to just cover the wet surface, so that the filling is now encased in dough. Lightly press down with the palm of your hand to seal. Lightly flour the sealed surface and roll the strip of filled dough over so the seam is on the bottom.

Use your hands as guides to make sure the long strip of filled dough is nice and straight. Using a large chef's knife, cut the strip into 6–8 pieces. Place each piece onto the prepared baking tray (cookie sheet), leaving approximately 3cm (1¼in) between each one. Brush the tops with water and sprinkle remaining 100g (1 cup) grated cheese evenly over the surface.

Cover loosely with clingfilm (plastic wrap) and leave to stand in a warm place for approximately 30 minutes. Remove clingfilm (plastic wrap) and place filled dough pieces in a preheated 230°C/450°F/Gas 8 oven, apply steam (page 44) and quickly close oven door. Bake for 20–25 minutes until golden brown. Remove from oven and place on a wire rack to cool slightly. Eat while warm.

Blue Cheese & Walnut Pavés

This is such a wonderful flavour combination in a simple bread dough. You might like to add a layer of sweet caramelised onion, too! I have even tried putting cold baked beans and cooked scrambled eggs inside before folding the bread dough over. It was simply amazing when eaten warm – like a breakfast bread pocket!

MAKES 6–8 PAVÉS

DOUGH
500g (3 cups) strong bread flour
10g (2 tsp) salt
20ml (4 tsp) olive oil
5g (1 tsp) sugar
7g (2½ tsp) instant dry yeast
350ml (1½ cups) water

FILLING
250g (9oz) strong blue cheese
150g (1½ cups) good-quality walnuts, roughly chopped

additional flour for dusting
50g (⅓ cup) sesame seeds, for topping

Place all dough ingredients except water in a large mixing bowl. Add water and, using a wooden spoon, combine to form a dough. Tip out onto a lightly floured surface and knead for 10–15 minutes, resting for 1 minute every 2–3 minutes, until dough is smooth and elastic.

Place dough in a lightly oiled large bowl, cover with clingfilm (plastic wrap) and leave in a warm place for 1 hour, until almost doubled in size. Tip dough onto floured work surface and gently deflate by folding it onto itself three or four times. Return dough to lightly oiled bowl and cover with clingfilm (plastic wrap). Leave a further 30 minutes in a warm place.

Gently tip dough onto a lightly floured work surface. Using a rolling pin, roll dough into a rectangle approximately 75cm long x 15cm wide (29in x 6in). Position dough rectangle on the work surface with long edge facing you. Crumble blue cheese and sprinkle chopped walnuts evenly over the dough, then fold the top edge of the dough over the filling to slightly over halfway. Using a pastry brush dipped in water, brush the surface of the folded dough. Fold the bottom dough edge with its filling upwards to just cover the wet surface, so that filling is now enclosed in dough. Lightly press down with the palm of your hand. Lightly flour the sealed surface and roll it over so the seam is on the bottom.

Use your hands as guides to make sure the long strip of filled dough is nice and straight. Using a large chef's knife, cut the strip into 6–8 pieces. Using a serrated knife, make 4–5 cuts on the top surface of the dough, all the way through to the filling.

Line a baking tray (cookie sheet) with baking (parchment) paper. Place each pavé onto the tray, leaving a 3cm (1¼in) gap between each one. Brush the tops with water and sprinkle sesame seeds evenly over the surface. Cover loosely with clingfilm (plastic wrap) and leave in a warm place for approximately 30 minutes.

Remove clingfilm (plastic wrap) and place tray in a preheated 230°C/450°F/Gas 8 oven. Apply steam (page 44) and close oven door quickly. Bake for 20–25 minutes until golden brown. Remove from oven and place on a wire rack to cool slightly. Eat while warm.

Carrot & Coriander Ciabatta

The secret of ciabatta is getting all that water properly absorbed into the flour and dough. I use a cake beater attachment for this dough as it is too wet to be mixed by hand or with a domestic mixer and dough hook. Making the biga (mother starter) overnight is key to the flavour, and the constant folding of the dough during fermentation is key to achieving that open, waxy, irregular texture that ciabatta is famous for. The carrot and coriander add a refreshing flavour and look.

MAKES 3–4 RECTANGULAR LOAVES

BIGA FERMENT
225g (1⅓ cups) strong bread flour
10g (1½ tbsp) wholemeal or whole wheat flour
10g (1½ tbsp) rye flour
1g (½ tsp) instant dry yeast
135ml (½ cup) water, chilled

DOUGH
300g (scant 2 cups) strong bread flour
3g (1 tsp) instant dry yeast
10g (2 tsp) salt
255ml (1 cup) water, chilled
1 quantity of Biga Ferment (from the day before)
75g (½ cup) grated carrot
15g (½ cup) fresh coriander (cilantro) leaves, finely chopped

additional flour for dusting

Make biga ferment a day in advance. Mix all ingredients together, then knead by hand until dough is elastic and a little smooth. Note the biga will be firm. Place dough in an oiled container, cover and leave to ferment overnight (18–24 hours) at room temperature.

The next day, place all dough ingredients except carrot and coriander (cilantro) in a mixer fitted with a cake beater attachment. Mix on low speed until a rough dough is formed. Continue to mix on medium speed until the dough is smooth, silky and almost fully developed; this should take approximately 7 minutes. In the last 2 minutes of mixing, add the carrot and coriander (cilantro). You may need to scrape down the beater and bowl from time to time to ensure all the dough is getting mixed.

Oil a rectangular container large enough for the dough to double in bulk. Place dough in container, cover with clingfilm (plastic wrap) and ferment for 20 minutes. Gently deflate dough by folding it onto itself 2–3 times, using plenty of flour for dusting in the container (see image 1). Rest dough for a further 20 minutes. Repeat deflating and resting dough for 20 minutes. Repeat a second time, deflating and resting dough for 30 minutes. You will notice that the dough has firmed up and is very gassy.

Turn dough out onto a well-floured work surface and, using a dough scraper, cut it into three or four rectangles (see image 2). Try to handle it as little as possible, as rough handling will result in loss of air and gas bubbles. Loosely roll each rectangle in flour so the top surface is covered in flour (see image 3). Dust a tea (dish) towel well with flour. Place dough pieces floured-surface up on the tea towel. Leave to rise for 30 minutes.

Line a baking tray (cookie sheet) with baking paper. Pick up each dough piece and gently stretch. Place onto the baking paper. Slide the dough with the baking paper directly onto a hot baking tray or baking stone in a preheated 230–240°C/450–475°F/Gas 8–9 oven. Create steam in the oven (page 44) and immediately close the oven door. Bake for 30–35 minutes or until golden brown and the bottoms sound hollow when tapped. Remove from oven and place on a wire rack to cool.

2

3

Brie & Caramelised Garlic Pain Miche

While filming my *Kiwi Baker in California* TV series at Della Fattoria in Petaluma, California, I spotted a half-eaten loaf of bread outside on a wooden table and couldn't resist digging in to it. It was a sourdough loaf with a wheel of Brie baked inside, topped with caramelised garlic. It was amazing! So here it is.

SERVES 8–10

1 large (at least 700g/1½lb) sourdough boule (page 58 – day-old is best)
1 large (15cm/6in) wheel of Brie or Camembert

CARAMELISED GARLIC TOPPING
3 garlic heads, separated into cloves
2 tbsp olive oil
2 tbsp water
1 tbsp balsamic vinegar
3 tbsp sugar
good pinch of salt
¼ tsp ground black pepper
1 sprig fresh rosemary, chopped

2–3 tbsp chopped parsley, to garnish

To make the caramelised garlic topping, blanch unpeeled garlic cloves in a saucepan of boiling water for 5 minutes, until just soft (test by pushing the tip of a sharp knife into the garlic; it should slide in easily). Refresh in cold water. Peel garlic and set aside.

Heat olive oil until shimmering in a heavy frying pan (skillet) over a medium heat. Add garlic and sauté for 1 minute, taking care not to burn. Add water and balsamic vinegar and as the mixture bubbles, add sugar, salt, pepper and rosemary. Reduce the heat to its lowest setting and simmer for 3–4 minutes until a syrup has formed and garlic is soft. Transfer to a bowl. Using a fork, mash the caramelised garlic to a spreadable paste that is a little rough in texture, not like a purée. Set aside until needed.

Place the Brie wheel on top of the loaf. Using a small sharp knife, cut around the outside circumference of the Brie, then remove it and set it aside. Cut a disc out of the loaf, about 5mm (¼in) deeper than the depth of the Brie. Place the Brie in the cavity in the loaf, then spread the caramelised garlic over the top.

Line a baking tray (cookie sheet) with baking (parchment) paper. Place loaf on prepared baking tray (cookie sheet). Bake in a preheated 220°C/425°F/Gas 7 oven for at least 20 minutes, until the loaf is crisp, the Brie is melted throughout and the caramelised garlic topping is bubbling. Remove loaf from oven and set aside for 15–20 minutes before cutting and serving – this is important, as the Brie will still be runny inside and super-hot! Sprinkle with chopped parsley and dig in.

Apple Cider Baton

The full fermented flavours of the dough (which must be prepared a day in advance) and the apple cider make this a standout bread at any dinner table. Shape it into rolls and serve with a tasty Cheddar cheese and a slice of crisp, fresh apple.

MAKES 2 BATONS

FERMENTED DOUGH

100g (⅔ cup) strong bread flour
pinch of salt
2g (scant 1 tsp) instant dry yeast
60ml (¼ cup) water

DOUGH

375g (2¼ cups) strong bread flour
75g (½ cup) wholemeal or whole wheat flour
50g (½ cup) rye flour
5g (1½ tsp) malt flour (enzyme-active malt flour is best)
10g (2 tsp) salt
3g (1 tsp) instant dry yeast
1 quantity of Fermented Dough (from the day before)
370ml (1½ cups) apple cider
275g (10oz) Granny Smith apples, peeled, cored and cut into 5mm (¼in) dice (keep in lemon water until needed)

additional flour for dusting

Begin the fermented dough a day in advance. In a bowl, mix all ingredients together to form a dough. Place on a work surface and knead for 8–10 minutes, until fully mixed (see page 29 on kneading dough). Place dough in a lightly oiled bowl, cover with clingfilm (plastic wrap) and leave overnight to ferment (12–16 hours).

The next day, place all dough ingredients except diced apple in a large mixing bowl. Using a wooden spoon, combine to form a dough mass. Tip dough out onto a lightly floured work surface and knead for around 15 minutes, resting it for 1 minute every 2–3 minutes, until dough is smooth and elastic. Pat diced apple pieces dry between kitchen paper (paper towels) and add to the dough. Very gently, incorporate the apple pieces into the dough, taking your time and being careful not to break up the apple pieces. When fully combined, place dough in a lightly oiled bowl, cover with clingfilm (plastic wrap) and leave in a warm place for 1 hour, until doubled in size.

Tip dough out onto the work surface and gently deflate by folding it onto itself three or four times. Return dough to the bowl, cover with clingfilm (plastic wrap) and leave in a warm place for 30 minutes, until dough is gassy and bubbly and full of life.

Gently tip dough onto lightly floured work surface and divide in half. Very gently and loosely shape dough pieces into a round ball. Cover with clingfilm (plastic wrap) and leave to rest for 20 minutes.

Lay a tea (dish) towel or proving cloth on a baking tray (cookie sheet) and dust with flour. Flatten each dough piece out, then tightly roll it up towards you like a pinwheel, applying pressure with your hands as you roll; the tighter the roll, the better (see page 37). Slightly taper the ends. Roll dough shapes in flour, then lay them seam-side up on the floured cloth, pleating the cloth in between so they are not touching in the final rising. Cover with plastic to prevent dough from drying out.

Leave to prove (rise) for 45–60 minutes, until three-quarters proved (risen) – use the indentation test (page 41) to tell when they are ready.

Place a baking tray (cookie sheet) or baking stone in the oven and preheat oven to 250°C/500°F/Gas 10. Line another baking tray (cookie sheet) with baking (parchment) paper.

Gently transfer both loaves seam-side down onto lined tray (sheet), keeping loaves at least 7cm (2¾in) apart. Using a razor blade or sharp knife, make lattice cuts in the top of each loaf. Slide the loaves, still on the baking (parchment) paper, onto the preheated tray (sheet) or baking stone. Apply steam in the oven (see page 44) then quickly close the oven door. Bake loaves for 20 minutes, then turn them around, reduce the oven temperature to 200°C/400°F/Gas 6 and bake for a further 15–20 minutes, until loaves are a dark golden-brown colour and the bottom sounds hollow when tapped. Place loaves on a wire rack to cool.

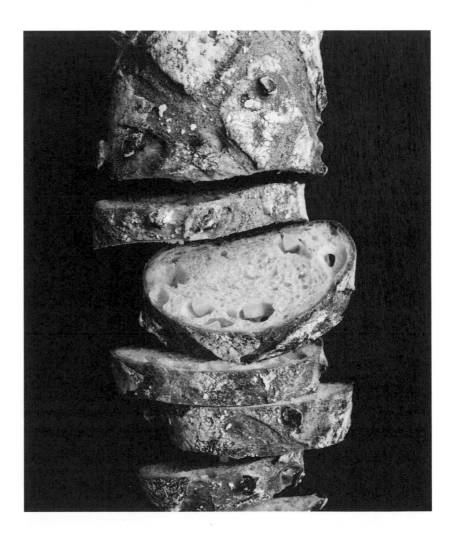

Marmite (Vegemite), Feta, Caramelised Onion & Tomato Rolls

The flavour combinations in these rolls are amazing, and you won't need to eat anything else after you've eaten one of these.

MAKES 12–15 ROLLS

DOUGH
400g (scant 2½ cups) strong bread flour
8g (1 heaping tsp) salt
5g (1¼ tsp) instant dry yeast
15ml (½ tbsp) olive oil
270ml (1 cup) water
additional flour for dusting

FILLING
20 cherry tomatoes
3–4 tbsp Marmite (Vegemite)
1 quantity of Caramelised Onion (page 193)
150g (5oz) feta (crumbly feta is best)

extra virgin olive oil, for brushing

Cut cherry tomatoes in half, season with salt and pepper, then roast in a preheated 100°C/212°F/Gas ¼ oven for 30 minutes.

Place flour, salt, yeast and oil in a large bowl and mix together. Add water and, using a wooden spoon, combine to form a dough. Tip dough out onto a lightly floured work surface and knead for 10–15 minutes, resting it for 1 minute every 2–3 minutes, until dough is smooth and elastic. Place in a lightly oiled bowl, cover with clingfilm (plastic wrap) and leave in a warm place for approximately 45 minutes, until almost doubled in size.

Tip dough onto the work surface and gently deflate by folding it onto itself three or four times. Return it to the bowl, cover with clingfilm (plastic wrap) and leave in a warm place for a further 30 minutes.

Line two baking trays (cookie sheets) with baking (parchment) paper. Soften Marmite (Vegemite) in microwave to spreading consistency.

Tip dough out onto a well-floured work surface and roll out to 35cm x 20cm (14in x 8in). Spread the softened Marmite (Vegemite), caramelised onion, roasted tomatoes and crumbled feta evenly over dough surface. Fold one third of the dough across the centre (see image 1), then fold the other third back over it so that you end up with a rectangle (see image 2). Gently press the dough with your fingertips to keep the ingredients together, and tuck the two open edges neatly under.

Using a large chef's knife, slice the dough crossways into 2cm (¾in) widths (see image 3). Lay dough slices cut-side up on the prepared trays (sheets), so you can see all the ingredients. Tuck any loose dough flaps under the dough. Cover with clingfilm (plastic wrap), place in a warm, draught-free place and leave to prove for approximately 30 minutes.

Bake rolls in a preheated 220°C/425°F/Gas 7 oven for 15–18 minutes, until golden brown. Remove from the oven, brush immediately with olive oil and place on a wire rack to cool.

Potato & Rosemary Focaccia

I bake this focaccia on the barbecue to give it a smoky flavour. It's really a cross between a focaccia and a thick-crust pizza. It's important to keep the dough a bit wet rather than too dry, to give the open, irregular crumb of a classic focaccia.

MAKES 1 LARGE FOCACCIA, SERVES 4–6

DOUGH
500g (3 cups) strong bread flour
10g (2 tsp) salt
30ml (2 tbsp) olive oil
15g (1 tbsp) sugar
5–10g (¼–⅓oz) fresh rosemary, chopped
7g (2½ tsp) instant dry yeast
380ml (1½ cups) water

TOPPINGS
200g (scant 1 cup) crème fraîche
2 cloves garlic, crushed
1 tbsp fresh rosemary, chopped
350g (12oz) medium potatoes, washed, skin on
4 tbsp olive oil
2 branches fresh rosemary, broken into sprigs
freshly ground salt and black pepper

Place all dough ingredients in a large mixing bowl and, using a wooden spoon, combine to form a dough.

Tip the dough out onto a lightly floured work surface and knead for 10–15 minutes, resting it for 1 minute every 2–3 minutes, until dough is smooth and elastic.

Put dough in a lightly oiled bowl large enough for dough to double in bulk. Cover with clingfilm (plastic wrap) and leave in a warm place for 1 hour. Tip dough onto the work surface and gently deflate by folding it onto itself three or four times. Return it to the bowl, cover with clingfilm (plastic wrap) and leave in a warm place for 30 minutes until dough has almost doubled in size.

Mix the crème fraîche, garlic and chopped rosemary in a bowl and set aside. Line a baking tray (cookie sheet) with baking (parchment) paper.

Tip dough out onto a well-floured work surface and, using your fingertips, very gently press out to a rectangle approximately 40cm x 30cm (16in x 12in). Don't press too heavily, as you need to retain the bubbles of gas in the dough. The dough will be elastic and it will take time to stretch it out to the desired shape. Carefully lift dough up and onto the prepared baking tray (cookie sheet) and give it a final gentle press with your fingertips to ensure it is even.

Spread the crème fraîche mixture over the entire surface of the dough. Using a mandoline slicer or a sharp knife, cut potatoes into super-thin slices, 1mm (⅓₂in) or finer, and arrange slices tightly and evenly over dough surface. Drizzle with oil, sprinkle with rosemary sprigs and season with freshly ground salt and pepper. Rest dough for 15 minutes.

Place baking tray (cookie sheet) in a preheated 250°C/500°F/Gas 10 oven and bake for 20–25 minutes, until the edges of the potatoes are crisp and browned, and the edges of the focaccia are very dark brown, almost burnt.

Remove from oven and leave to cool for 5 minutes, then slide focaccia onto a large wooden chopping (cutting) board, cut into slices and devour immediately.

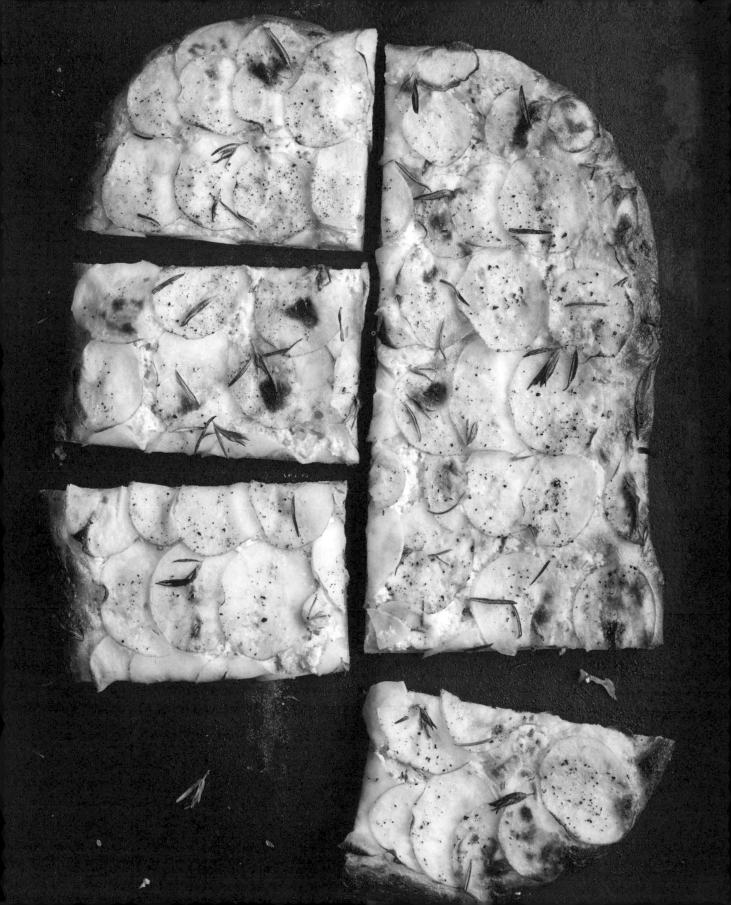

Grainy & Healthy Breads

German Vollkorn Bread

This is our number one selling loaf of bread among the Asian locals and expats alike at my artisan bakery Baker & Cook, in Singapore. It's a healthy loaf that is good for sandwiches and toast. It has great keeping qualities, and is not as heavy and dense as the Danish Rugbrød (see page 101).

MAKES 1 LOAF

SOAKED GRAINS

25g (5 tsp) kibbled wheat grains
25g (5 tsp) kibbled rye grains
25g (5 tsp) whole barley grains
20g (2 tbsp) chia grains
20g (¼ cup) jumbo rolled oats
50g (⅓ cup) sunflower seeds
20g (2 tbsp) linseeds (flaxseeds)
15g (1¾ tbsp) coarse corn grits or coarse polenta (cornmeal)
15g (1 heaping tbsp) sesame seeds
150ml (⅔ cup) hot water

DOUGH

400g (scant 2½ cups) strong bread flour
1 quantity of Soaked Grains (from the day before)
8g (1 heaping tsp) salt
10g (1½ tsp) honey
5g (1¼ tsp) instant dry yeast
5g (1 tbsp) cocoa powder
10ml (2 tsp) olive oil
300ml (1¼ cups) water

additional flour for dusting
100g (1 cup) jumbo rolled oats, to decorate

Prepare the soaked grains a day in advance by placing all ingredients in a bowl and mixing together. Cover and leave to soak overnight (12–16 hours).

The next day, place all dough ingredients in a large mixing bowl. Using a wooden spoon, combine to form a dough. Tip dough out onto a lightly floured surface and knead for 15 minutes, resting it for 1 minute every 2–3 minutes, until dough is smooth and elastic. The dough will be sticky to the touch at first. It's okay to add a little extra flour during the kneading process, but don't be tempted to add excessive amounts.

Lightly oil a bowl large enough to allow dough to double in bulk. Put dough in bowl and cover with clingfilm (plastic wrap). Leave in a warm place for 1 hour. Gently knock back dough in bowl by folding it back onto itself: this will deflate it slightly, but it will develop more strength. Cover again with clingfilm (plastic wrap) and leave for 30 minutes.

Tip dough out onto a lightly floured work surface and gently mould into a roundish shape. Cover with clingfilm (plastic wrap) and rest for 15 minutes.

Remove clingfilm (plastic wrap) and flatten dough, then mould into a rectangular loaf shape (page 36). Wet loaf by brushing all over with a pastry brush dipped in water, then roll it in rolled oats to coat evenly all over. Grease a 19cm x 11cm x 11cm-(7½in x 4½in x 4½in-)deep loaf tin (pan). Place loaf seam-side down in tin (pan). Using a sharp knife, make a deep cut lengthways down centre of loaf. Cover with clingfilm (plastic wrap) and leave to prove (rise) for 45 minutes to 1 hour.

Place loaf tin in a preheated 240°C/475°F/Gas 9 oven, add steam (page 44) and quickly close oven door. Bake for approximately 20 minutes, then lower oven temperature to 200°C/400°F/Gas 6 and bake for a further 30 minutes, or until bottom of loaf sounds hollow when tapped with your knuckles. Remove loaf from oven and turn out onto a wire rack to cool.

Dark Beer, Walnut & Cranberry Rolls

These small rolls with sweet or savoury filings are great at any time of the day. They are packed full of flavour. The richness of the dark malt beer works really well with the walnuts and cranberries, with a hint of honey for sweetness. Serve them at the start of a meal, or with cheese at the end.

MAKES 15 ROLLS

400g (scant 2½ cups) strong bread flour

100g (⅔ cup) wholemeal or whole wheat flour

8g (2¾ tsp) instant dry yeast

10g (2 tsp) salt

30g (1½ tbsp) treacle (blackstrap molasses)

20g (1 tbsp) honey

20ml (4 tsp) olive oil

330ml (1⅓ cups) dark malt beer

150g (1½ cups) walnut pieces, chopped into small pieces

150g (1¼ cups) dried cranberries, roughly chopped

Place all ingredients except walnuts and cranberries in a large mixing bowl. Using a wooden spoon, combine ingredients to form a dough. Tip dough out onto a lightly floured work surface and knead for 15 minutes, resting for 1 minute every 2–3 minutes, until dough is smooth and elastic. Add walnuts and cranberries and knead gently until well incorporated.

Place dough in a lightly oiled bowl, cover with clingfilm (plastic wrap) and leave in a warmish place (23–25°C/73–77°F) for approximately 1½ hours, until dough has doubled in size. Gently knock back dough in bowl by folding dough back onto itself several times. Cover again and leave for a further 30 minutes.

Gently tip dough onto a lightly floured work surface and divide into 15 equal pieces, approximately 80g (3oz) each. Roll each into a small ball or bun shape (page 39).

Line a baking tray (cookie sheet) with baking (parchment) paper. Roll the rolls in flour and place them on baking tray (cookie sheet), leaving a 2–3cm (¾–1¼in) gap between each roll. Using a razor blade or sharp knife, make little decorative cuts in the rolls; these will expand during proving. Cover with clingfilm (plastic wrap) and leave for 45–60 minutes until almost fully proved.

Place baking tray (cookie sheet) in a preheated 230°C/450°F/Gas 8 oven, apply steam (page 44) and close door quickly. Bake for 20–25 minutes, turning tray (sheet) around halfway through baking if needed. Remove rolls from oven and place on a wire rack to cool.

Gluten-free Bread

I've added some variations to the basic recipe for gluten-free bread, but the additions and combinations are endless – it's up to your imagination.

MAKES 1 LARGE (1KG) LOAF OR 2 SMALLER (500G/1LB 2OZ) LOAVES

460g (3 cups) rice flour (or 360g (2¼ cups) white rice flour and 100g (⅔ cup) brown rice flour)

2 tbsp guar gum or xanthan gum

20g (1¾ tbsp) soft brown sugar

1½ tsp salt

40g (¼ cup) fine polenta (cornmeal)

7g (2½ tsp) instant dry yeast

350ml (1½ cups) soy milk

100ml (scant ½ cup) water

45ml (3 tbsp) vegetable oil

3 eggs

1 tsp cider vinegar

½ tbsp sesame seeds, for topping
½ tbsp poppy seeds, optional, for topping

Put all the dry ingredients in a large bowl and stir with a wooden spoon to combine evenly. Make a well in the middle.

Place remaining ingredients (except the seeds) in a separate bowl and stir with a wooden spoon to combine evenly.

Pour wet ingredients into the well in the dry ingredients and mix gently with a wooden spoon to form a firm and slightly elastic dough. If dough is too stiff to mix with a wooden spoon, use your hand: put some elbow grease into the mixing!

Grease a 1kg (2¼lb) loaf tin (pan) or two 500g (1lb 2oz) loaf tins (pans). Tip dough into greased tin (pan) or tins (pans), smooth top with a spoon or spatula and sprinkle surface with sesame and poppy seeds (if desired). Cover with clingfilm (plastic wrap) and leave to prove in a warm place for 1 hour, or until dough has risen to approximately 1.5cm (⅝in)below the top of the tin.

Place tins (pans) in a preheated 220°C/425°F/Gas 7 oven, add steam (page 44) and close door quickly. Bake for 20–25 minutes, or until bottom of loaf sounds hollow when tapped with your knuckles. Remove from oven and cool on a wire rack.

VARIATIONS: Spicy Fruit & Nut Loaf – Add 2 teaspoons mixed spice, 100g (½ cup) sultanas (golden raisins) and 100g (⅔ cup) chopped lightly roasted walnuts; mix in with the dry ingredients. Omit the sesame and poppy seed topping. Bake as above.

Italian-style Loaf – Mix in 2 teaspoons of dried mixed herbs or oregano with the dry ingredients. Mix in 100g (3½oz) chopped sundried tomatoes and 100g (½ cup) chopped black olives with the wet ingredients. Omit the sesame and poppy seed topping. Bake as above. Brush top surface of loaf with olive oil immediately it comes out of the oven.

Cheese & Bacon Loaf – Mix in 75g (½ cup) diced onion, 100g (¾ cup) cooked diced bacon and 75g (¾ cup) grated cheese with the wet ingredients. Sprinkle top surface of loaf with grated cheese instead of seeds before baking. Bake as above.

Vine Fruit, Treacle & Rosemary Sourdough

This magical flavour combination has been a favourite of mine since Phillippa Grogan from Phillippa's Breads, Pastries and Provisions in Melbourne, Australia introduced it to me over 15 years ago. I've gone one step further and added treacle for a little sweetness. It makes a perfect partner to any cheese. I smile every time I smell this loaf.

MAKES 3 LOAVES

SOAKED GRAINS

15g (3 tsp) kibbled wheat

15g (3 tsp) kibbled rye

15g (1½ tbsp) jumbo rolled oats

15g (1¾ tbsp) sunflower seeds

15g (1½ tbsp) linseeds (flaxseeds)

15g (1¾ tbsp) coarse corn grits or coarse polenta (cornmeal)

70ml (¼ cup) hot water

DOUGH

1 quantity of Soaked Grains (from the day before)

450g (2¾ cups) strong bread flour

50g (½ cup) rye flour

100g (3½oz) Sourdough Levain Starter (page 186) – healthy, live and fed at least 8 hours before using

5g (1½ tsp) malt flour (enzyme-active is best)

10g (2 tsp) salt

3g (1 tsp) instant dry yeast

20g (¾oz) fresh rosemary, roughly chopped

240ml (1 cup) (approx.) chilled water

230g (1⅓ cups) plumped sultanas (golden raisins) (from the day before)

additional flour for dusting

Prepare the soaked grains a day ahead by placing all ingredients into a bowl and mixing together. Cover and soak overnight for 12–16 hours. Wash the sultanas in hot water and leave to drain in a sieve overnight.

The next day, place all dough ingredients except sultanas in a large mixing bowl and, using a wooden spoon, combine to form a dough mass.

Tip dough out onto a lightly floured work surface and knead for around 15 minutes, resting it for 1 minute every 2–3 minutes, until dough is smooth and elastic. Add sultanas and very gently incorporate into the dough, taking your time and being careful not to mash the sultanas into pieces. Place dough in a lightly oiled bowl, cover with clingfilm (plastic wrap) and leave in a warm place for about 3 hours, until dough has almost doubled in size. Tip dough onto the work surface and gently deflate by folding it onto itself three or four times. Return dough to bowl, cover with clingfilm (plastic wrap) and leave a further 1 hour in a warm place, until dough is really gassy and bubbly and full of energy.

Gently tip dough onto a lightly floured work surface, divide it into three equal pieces and very gently and loosely shape into round balls. Cover with clingfilm (plastic wrap) and rest for 20 minutes.

While dough is resting, lay a tea (dish) towel or proving cloth on a baking tray (cookie sheet) and dust with flour. Uncover the dough rounds and mould dough pieces into their final baton shape (see page 37). Slightly taper the ends.

Lay the first loaf seam-side down onto the floured cloth. Before laying the next loaf beside it, pleat the cloth in between so the loaves don't touch each other in the final rising. Cover with clingfilm (plastic wrap).

Prove (rise) the loaves for 45–60 minutes, until three-quarters proved. Use the indentation test (page 41) to tell when they are ready: the dough should spring back slightly when pressed.

Line a baker's peel or a flat oven tray with baking (parchment) paper. Gently transfer the loaves seam-side down onto baking paper, leaving a gap of at least 7cm (2¾in) between the loaves. Using a razor blade or sharp knife, make one long cut down the centre, with the blade on a 45° angle. Slide the loaves, still on the baking (parchment) paper, onto a baking tray (cookie sheet) or stone preheated in a 250°C/500°F/Gas 10 oven. Apply steam in the oven (page 44) and quickly close the oven door.

Bake loaves for 20 minutes, then rotate them for even baking, reduce the oven temperature to 200°C/400°F/Gas 6 and bake for a further 10–15 minutes or until a dark golden brown, and the bottom of the loaves sound hollow when tapped with your knuckles. Place on a wire rack to cool.

Farmhouse Wholemeal Loaf

There is nothing like a healthy wholemeal bread – sometimes called whole wheat bread – in a classic loaf shape. If you want to make a denser loaf, reduce the white flour and increase the wholemeal flour proportionally.

MAKES 2 LOAVES

250g (1½ cups) strong bread flour

250g (1½ cups) wholemeal or whole wheat flour

10g (2 tsp) salt

10g (2 heaping tsp) sugar

8g (2¾ tsp) instant dry yeast

20ml (4 tsp) olive oil

380ml (1½ cups) water

additional flour for dusting

100g (scant 1 cup) wheatgerm or wheat bran, for coating the loaf

Place all ingredients in a large mixing bowl. Using a wooden spoon, combine to form a dough. Tip dough out onto a lightly floured surface and knead for 15–20 minutes, resting it for 1 minute every 2–3 minutes, until smooth and elastic. The dough will be sticky to the touch at first; it's okay to add a little extra flour during the kneading process, but don't be tempted to add excessive amounts.

Lightly oil a bowl large enough for dough to double in bulk. Put dough in bowl and cover with clingfilm (plastic wrap). Leave in a warm place for 1 hour. Gently knock back dough in the bowl by folding it back onto itself – this will deflate it slightly, but it will develop more strength. Cover dough again with clingfilm (plastic wrap) and leave for 30 minutes.

Tip dough out onto a lightly floured work surface and divide into two equal pieces. Gently shape each piece into a roundish shape. Cover with clingfilm (plastic wrap) and leave to rest for 15 minutes.

Flatten and mould each dough piece into a rectangular loaf shape (page 36). Wet each loaf entirely using a pastry brush dipped in water, then roll in wheatgerm or wheat bran to give an even coating. Using a sharp knife or razor blade, make three diagonal cuts in the top of each loaf.

Grease two 500g (1lb 2oz) loaf tins (pans). Place loaves in tins (pans), cover with clingfilm (plastic wrap) and prove for 1 hour.

Place loaves in a preheated 230°C/450°F/Gas 8 oven, apply steam (page 44) and quickly close oven door. Bake for 25–30 minutes or until bottom of loaf sounds hollow when tapped with your finger. Remove loaves from oven and turn out onto a wire rack to cool.

Muesli Rolls

These are a real breakfast roll for champions, full of seeds, dried fruits and chocolate. They are great fresh, or toasted the next day. Try them with a Swiss Emmental cheese – perfect bread and breakfast partners!

MAKES 15 ROLLS

450g (2¾ cups) strong bread flour

50g (⅓ cup) wholemeal or whole wheat flour

40g (½ cup) jumbo rolled oats

8g (2¾ tsp) instant dry yeast

10g (2 tsp) salt

30g (1½ tbsp) treacle (blackstrap molasses)

20g (1 tbsp) honey

20ml (4 tsp) olive oil

370ml (1½ cups) water

40g (scant ½ cup) walnut pieces, chopped into small pieces

30g (3 tbsp) linseeds (flaxseeds)

20g (2¼ tbsp) sesame seeds

80g (½ cup) sunflower seeds

80g (⅔ cup) pumpkin seeds

40g (⅓ cup) dried cranberries

40g (¼ cup) dried apricots, cut into pieces

80g (½ cup) small chocolate drops or chocolate chips, optional

100g (1 generous cup) jumbo rolled oats, to decorate

Place flours, oats, yeast, salt and wet ingredients in a large mixing bowl. Using a wooden spoon, combine to form a dough. Tip dough out onto a lightly floured surface and knead for 15 minutes, resting it for 1 minute every 2–3 minutes, until dough is smooth and elastic. Check dough throughout kneading for stickiness: add a little more water or flour if necessary to achieve a soft dough that's not too firm.

Add walnuts, seeds, dried fruit and chocolate (if desired). Knead until well incorporated and combined into dough. Place dough in a lightly oiled bowl, cover with clingfilm (plastic wrap) and leave in a warm place for approximately 1½ hours, until dough has doubled in size. Gently knock back dough in bowl by folding it back onto itself several times. Cover again and leave for a further 30 minutes.

Tip dough upside down onto a lightly floured work surface. Sprinkle flour over top of dough (which was on the bottom of the bowl). Very carefully turn dough over, and gently flatten to 2cm (¾in) thick. Using a dough scraper or large chef's knife, cut dough into 7cm (2¾in) squares. Using a pastry brush, brush the tops with water. Sprinkle entire surface of each roll with rolled oats, and pat down gently to stick them on.

Line a baking tray (cookie sheet) with baking (parchment) paper. Place rolls onto lined tray (sheet), leaving a 2–3cm (¾–1¼in) gap between each roll. Cover with clingfilm (plastic wrap) and leave to prove for 30–45 minutes, depending on room temperature (see indentation test, page 41).

Place rolls on baking tray (cookie sheet) in a preheated 230°C/450°F/ Gas 8 oven, apply steam (page 44) and quickly close oven door. Bake for 20–25 minutes, turning tray around halfway through baking if needed. Remove rolls from oven and place on a wire rack to cool.

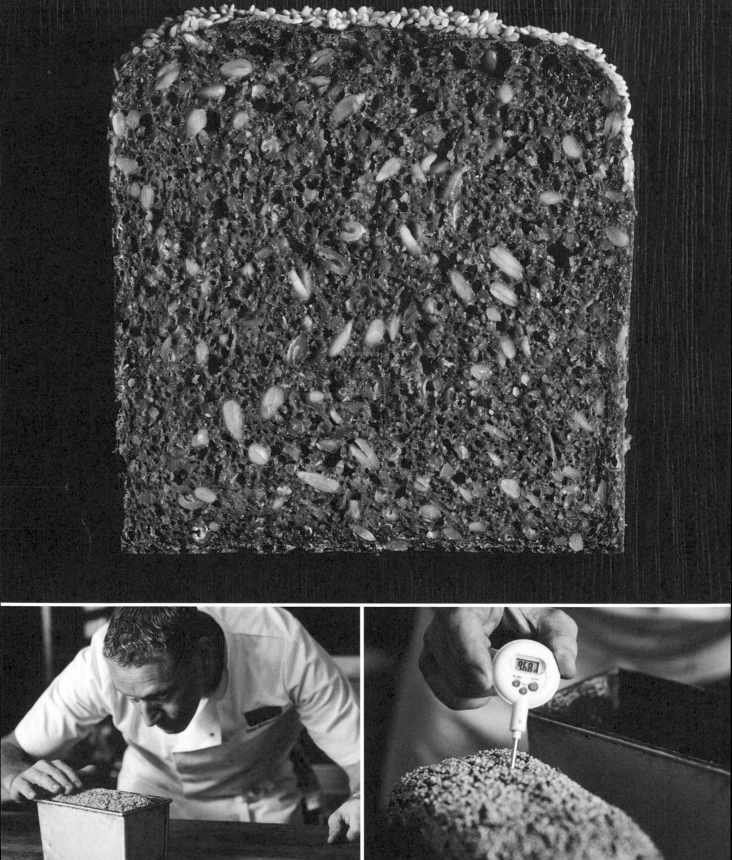

Danish Rugbrød with Sunflower Seeds

This is a trendy, healthy bread full of grains. Whole wheatberries or grains are nutritious and slow to release their goodness, which is better for the body. This is the perfect bread for Danish Smørrebrød or open sandwich. It's great with cold meats, too – or with raspberry jam and Nutella.

MAKES 1 LOAF

SOAKED GRAINS

215g (1 cup) whole rye grains (or whole wheat or kibbled grain, or a mixture of both)

150g (1 cup) sunflower seeds, lightly toasted if desired

15g (1 tbsp) salt

300ml (1¼ cups) hot water

DOUGH

200g (scant 1¼ cups) strong bread flour

100g (1 cup) rye flour, coarsely ground (stoneground is best)

10g (2 tsp) liquid malt extract or molasses

15g (2¾ tbsp) cocoa powder

20ml (4 tsp) olive oil

100g (3½oz) Quick Rye Sourdough (page 190) – must be made 24 hours or more in advance

150ml (⅔ cup) warm water (approx. 30°C/86°F)

½ tsp instant dry yeast

75g (½ cup) grated carrot

1 quantity of Soaked Grains (from the day before)

50g (⅓ cup) sesame seeds or 50g (½ cup) rye flour, for topping (optional)

Prepare the soaked grains in advance. Place all ingredients in a bowl and mix to coat grains with water. Cover and leave at room temperature for 16–24 hours.

Place all dough ingredients in a mixer fitted with a beater. Mix on medium speed for 10 minutes, scraping down the sides of the bowl occasionally for an even mix. Alternatively, you can mix by hand using a large metal spoon. This will take some effort as the dough is like a stiff fruitcake batter.

Grease a 19cm x 11cm x 11cm-(7½in x 4½in x 4½in-)deep loaf tin (pan). Once the batter is mixed, spoon it into the loaf tin (pan). Using your knuckles dipped in water, squash the batter into the corners of the tin (pan), then smooth it out with a spatula or scraper until level and smooth. Sprinkle sesame seeds on top, if desired.

Alternatively, scrape the dough out onto a work surface heavily sprinkled with rye flour. Roll dough into a fat log shape, 2cm (¾in) narrower than the width of the tin (pan). Place dough log in greased tin (pan) and dust top of loaf with rye flour.

Cover tin loosely with clingfilm (plastic wrap) and leave to rise for 2½–3 hours. Do not leave for longer than this, as the dough will collapse if it is over-proved. In the last 30–45 minutes of the rising, preheat oven to 250°C/450°F/Gas 8.

Remove clingfilm (plastic wrap) and place loaf in preheated oven. Immediately lower oven temperature to 180°C/350°F/Gas 4, then add steam (page 44) and close oven door quickly. Bake for 60–70 minutes or until the internal temperature of the loaf is 95°C (203°F), using a temperature probe.

Remove from oven and leave to set in the tin (pan) for 5 minutes before turning out onto a wire rack to cool. Leave for at least 5–6 hours, or preferably overnight, wrapped in a clean tea (dish) towel, before slicing. If the loaf is not cooled correctly before slicing, the internal texture will not have set correctly and the knife will 'gum up' with what seems like unbaked dough.

Rye & Caraway Bread

I first experienced this special bread when I was in New York eating a sandwich at a typical Jewish deli. Caraway seed is an acquired taste – either you like it or you don't. If you don't, simply leave it out. The cocoa powder is added to darken the crumb colour: if you want a light rye bread, leave it out. Try this bread thickly sliced with pulled pork and caramelised onion to make an amazing sandwich.

MAKES 1 LARGE LOAF

350g (generous 2 cups) strong bread flour
150g (1½ cups) rye flour (coarsely ground is best)
10g (2 tsp) salt
10g (2 heaping tsp) sugar
7g (2½ tsp) instant dry yeast
10ml (2 tsp) olive oil
15g (2¾ tbsp) cocoa powder
10g (1½ tsp) molasses
20g (3 tbsp) caraway seeds
340ml (1⅓ cups) water
additional flour for dusting

Place all dry ingredients in a large mixing bowl. Add water and, using a wooden spoon, combine to form a dough. Tip dough out onto a lightly floured surface and knead for 10–15 minutes, resting it for 30 seconds every 2–3 minutes, until dough is smooth and elastic.

Lightly oil a bowl large enough to allow dough to double in bulk. Put dough in bowl and cover with clingfilm (plastic wrap). Leave in a warm place for 1 hour. Gently knock back the dough in the bowl by folding it back onto itself; this will deflate the dough slightly, but it will develop more strength. Cover again with clingfilm (plastic wrap) and leave for 30 minutes.

Gently tip dough onto a lightly floured work surface, and very gently mould it into a round ball shape. Cover and leave to rest for 15–20 minutes. Meanwhile, lay a clean tea (dish) towel inside a large, round cane basket or bowl. Heavily dust the tea (dish) towel with flour to create an even layer of flour. If you have a coiled cane banneton, dust it heavily with flour. Make sure the basket is large enough for the dough to double in size.

Mould dough into its final round ball shape, making sure the ball is tight and firm and the seam is at the bottom. Gently place in the flour-dusted basket or bowl seam-side down and smooth surface facing upwards. Cover with plastic. Leave in a warm place for approximately 60 minutes or until the dough is three-quarters proved (risen) – the dough will spring back a little when pressed with your finger (see page 41).

Preheat oven to 250°C/500°F/Gas 10, with a baking tray (cookie sheet) inside. Remove the preheated tray (sheet) and gently tip dough onto it, seam-side facing upwards. Lightly dust the loaf with flour. Place tray (sheet) immediately back into the oven, create steam in the oven (page 44) and quickly close the oven door. Bake for 20 minutes. Turn tray (sheet) around for even baking, reduce oven temperature to 200°C/400°F/Gas 6 and bake for a further 20 minutes or until loaf is a dark golden brown, and when bottom of loaf is tapped it sounds hollow. Remove from oven and place on a wire rack to cool.

Danish Rye & Chocolate Boller

These are all the craze with children in Scandinavia. They are the perfect snack – a little bit of chocolate with a whole bunch of wholegrain. That's a sneaky way to get children to eat healthily. Prepare the soaked grains 16–24 hours in advance.

MAKES 16 ROLLS

SOAKED GRAINS

200g (1 cup) whole rye grains (or whole wheat or kibbled grain, or a mixture of both)

75g (½ cup) sunflower seeds, lightly toasted if desired

75g (⅔ cup) pumpkin seeds

50g (¼ cup) linseeds (flaxseeds)

15g (1 tbsp) salt

300ml (1¼ cups) hot water

DOUGH

200g (scant 1¼ cups) strong bread flour

100g (1 cup) rye flour, coarsely ground (stoneground is best)

10g (2 tsp) liquid malt extract or molasses

20g (3¾ tbsp) cocoa powder

20ml (4 tsp) olive oil

100g (3½oz) Quick Rye Sourdough (page 190) – must be made at least 24 hours in advance

130ml (½ cup) warm water (approx. 30°C/86°F)

¼ tsp instant dry yeast

1 quantity of Soaked Grains (from the day before)

100g (3½oz) chocolate buttons or pieces

200g (1⅔ cups) pumpkin seeds, for topping

Prepare the soaked grains a day in advance. Place all ingredients in a bowl and mix to coat with the water. Cover and stand at room temperature for 16–24 hours.

The next day, grease two standard-sized muffin pans with non-stick baking spray or butter.

Place all dough ingredients into a mixer fitted with a beater. Mix on medium speed for 10 minutes, scraping down the sides of the bowl and the beater occasionally for an even mix. Alternatively, mix by hand using a large metal spoon. This will take some effort as the dough is like a very stiff fruitcake batter.

Spoon approximately 85g (3oz) of mixture into your hand and roll into a rough ball. Roll ball in pumpkin seeds and place into a greased muffin hole. Very gently pat the dough into the muffin hole – do not flatten it too much. Alternatively, place the rolls directly onto a baking tray (cookie sheet) lined with baking (parchment) paper and press down a little with the palm of your hand. Cover loosely with clingfilm (plastic wrap) and leave to rise for 1½–2 hours. In the last 30–45 minutes of rising, preheat oven to 240°C/475°F/Gas 9.

Place muffin pans or baking tray (cookie sheet) in preheated oven. Immediately lower oven temperature to 180°C/350°F/Gas 4, then add steam (page 44) and quickly close oven door. Bake for 30–35 minutes. Remove from oven and leave rolls to set in trays (sheets) for 5 minutes before turning out onto a wire rack. Leave to cool for a few hours before eating.

Quick Breads & Scones

Wholemeal Soda Bread

This is a classic quick bread with simple ingredients. It is good with a hearty winter soup; or serve at a picnic spread with pure creamy butter and topped with ham, summer vegetables and your favourite chutney. You can also add ingredients such as sundried tomatoes, mixed herbs, olives or walnuts to create your own special soda bread. Best eaten within a day of baking.

MAKES 1 LOAF

250g (1⅔ cups) plain white (all-purpose) flour

250g (1½ cups) wholemeal or whole wheat flour

1 tsp bicarbonate of soda (baking soda)

1 tsp salt

400ml (1⅔ cups) buttermilk

Place dry ingredients in a large mixing bowl and mix well to combine. If you are adding other ingredients (see variations below), add at this stage. Stir in buttermilk and mix to form a rough, sticky dough ball. Don't over-mix dough at this stage as it will make the soda bread tough.

Tip dough out onto a lightly floured work surface and shape into a ball or cob shape. Flatten it slightly with the palm of your hand. Transfer to a baking tray (cookie sheet) lined with baking (parchment) paper. Using a large chef's knife or dough scraper, cut a deep cross three-quarters of the way through the dough ball. Dust with flour and leave to rest for 10 minutes.

Place tray (sheet) in a preheated 210°C/410°F/Gas 6½ oven. Bake for approximately 30 minutes, or until bottom of loaf sounds hollow when tapped with your knuckles. Remove from oven and place on a wire rack to cool.

VARIATIONS: Make your own buttermilk by mixing to combine 200g (scant 1 cup) natural yoghurt, 200ml (scant 1 cup) whole milk and a squeeze of lemon juice.

Vary the soda bread by adding your choice of grated Cheddar, olives, sundried tomatoes, herbs, dried fruits or nuts just before mixing in the buttermilk.

Classic Date Scone with Raspberry Jam & Cream

These scones are light and fluffy. If you can get hold of Cornish clotted cream to replace the Cream Chantilly, even better! If you don't like dates, replace them with sultanas (golden raisins), or leave the scones plain.

MAKES 12 SCONES

500g (3⅓ cups) plain (all-purpose) flour

25g (1 heaping tbsp) baking powder

good pinch of salt

80g (scant ½ cup) caster (superfine) sugar

85g (⅓ cup) butter, softened

250g (9oz) dates, chopped (or sultanas)

1 egg

150ml (⅔ cup) milk

130g (½ cup) natural yoghurt

1 egg whisked with 20ml (4 tsp) milk, for egg wash

Homemade Raspberry Jam (page 193) – or good-quality store-bought jam

Cream Chantilly (page 192) – or clotted cream

Preheat oven to 220°C/425°F/Gas 7 and make sure oven rack is on the middle shelf. Line a baking tray (cookie sheet) with baking (parchment) paper.

Sift flour, baking powder, salt and sugar into a large mixing bowl. Add softened butter and rub in with your fingertips until mixture resembles breadcrumbs. Add chopped dates and, using your fingers, lift dates through mixture to incorporate.

In a jug (pitcher), lightly combine egg, milk and yoghurt with a fork. Add wet ingredients to dry ingredients and, using a wooden spoon, gently mix together to form a dough that is a little soft and sticky. Make sure all ingredients are well combined.

Tip dough out onto a floured work surface and sprinkle a little flour on top. Pat dough out to a rough rectangle and fold it in half, then turn dough 90 degrees and repeat the patting down and folding. You will notice the dough becoming smoother. Be careful not to over-work the dough.

Roll dough out on a floured work surface to a rectangle approximately 3cm (1¼in) thick. Using a large chef's knife or a dough scraper, cut dough into 6cm (2½in) squares. Place scones on prepared baking tray (cookie sheet), leaving a 2–3cm (¾–1¼in) gap between each scone so they don't touch. Leave to rest for a few minutes to let the baking powder work. Using a pastry brush, brush the tops of the scones with egg wash. Take care to glaze only the tops; if egg wash runs down the sides it will stop the scones from rising evenly.

Place scones on middle shelf in preheated oven and bake for 15–20 minutes, until scones have risen and are golden brown. Leave on tray to cool.

To serve, split scones in half, spread with butter and add raspberry jam and Cream Chantilly or clotted cream.

Spinach, Pumpkin, Cumin & Feta Damper

This is an old favourite of mine but with a new twist – toasted cumin seeds – to create a damper packed full of flavour. You can bake damper in a barbecue: just raise the baking tray (cookie sheet) a few centimetres above the grill so the damper doesn't burn on the bottom.

MAKES 3 DAMPER LOAVES

500g (3 cups) strong bread flour

5g (1 tsp) salt

40g (2 heaping tbsp) baking powder

65g (¼ cup) unsalted butter, softened

good pinch of freshly ground black pepper

10g (1 heaping tbsp) cumin seeds, lightly toasted

350ml (1½ cups) whole milk, tepid

120g (4oz) feta, roughly cubed

100g (3½oz) spinach, washed, dried and roughly chopped

100g (3½oz) firm cooked pumpkin, cubed

Sift flour, salt, and baking powder into a large mixing bowl. Add butter and, using your fingertips, rub butter into dry ingredients until mixture resembles breadcrumbs. Toss black pepper and cumin seeds through. Make a large well in the mixture and slowly add the milk into the well. Gently combine ingredients by hand, taking care not to over-mix.

Once dough is almost fully combined, but still has some wet and floury patches throughout, add the feta, spinach and pumpkin. Fold and lift into the dough to give a rough dough mass. Do not over-mix dough at this stage as it would result in a tough damper.

Tip dough out onto work surface and divide into three equal parts. Very lightly mould each piece into a round shape and place smooth side up on a baking tray (cookie sheet) lined with baking (parchment) paper. Gently flatten each dough piece to a 15cm-(6in-)diameter circle, using the palm of your hand. Lightly dust with flour, then leave to rest in a cool place for 15 minutes.

Using a large knife or dough scraper, score each dough piece into quarters, cutting three-quarters of the way through the dough. Bake in a preheated 220–230°C/425–450°F/Gas 7–8 oven for 18–25 minutes, depending on size. Do not over-bake as this will result in a dry damper. Remove from oven and place on a wire rack to cool.

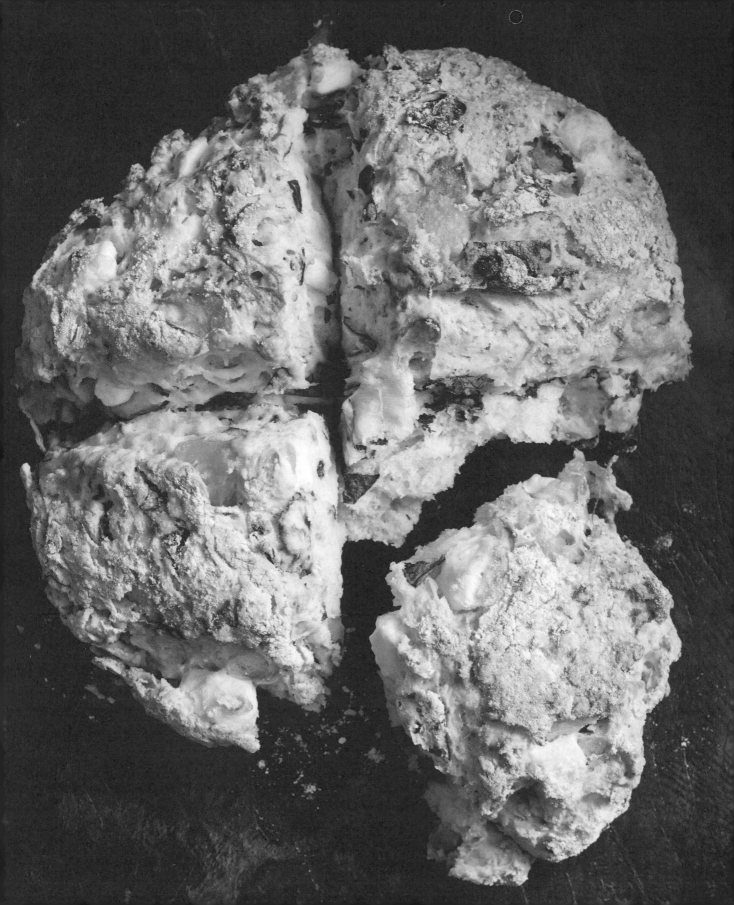

Garden Vegetable, Cheese & Hidden Egg Savoury Muffins

I love the fact that there is a hidden surprise in the middle of these savoury muffins. They are great at breakfast time, served slightly warm so the egg is still a little runny.

MAKES 6 LARGE MUFFINS

6 small eggs

300g (2 cups) plain (all-purpose) flour

18g (3 heaping tsp) baking powder

5g (1 tsp) salt

20g (1¾ tbsp) sugar

¼ tsp cayenne pepper

100g (1 cup) tasty cheese, grated

20g (¾oz) red onion, finely diced

20g (2 heaping tbsp) sweetcorn kernels, drained

20g (scant ¼ cup) red (bell) pepper, finely diced

20g (scant ¼ cup) courgette (zucchini), grated

20g (scant ¼ cup) carrot, grated

1 tbsp finely chopped parsley

½ red chilli, finely chopped

20 kalamata or black olives, pitted and chopped

½ tbsp poppy seeds

2 small eggs for batter

250ml (1 cup) whole milk

50ml (scant ¼ cup) vegetable oil

100g (1 cup) tasty cheese, grated, for topping

6 cherry tomatoes, sliced thinly, for topping

Preheat oven to 200°C/400°F/Gas 6. Butter six muffin holes (or spray with non-stick vegetable oil) and set aside.

To boil the six eggs, three-quarters fill a small saucepan with water and bring it to a fast boil. Add a good pinch of salt. Using a spoon, lower eggs into the water slowly, so the shells don't crack. Boil for 5 minutes for a soft-centred egg. Cool eggs in cold running water for 3–4 minutes. Carefully peel eggs and set aside.

Sift dry ingredients together in a large bowl. Add first measure of grated cheese, vegetables, parsley, chilli, olives and poppy seeds. Toss together.

Break the two eggs into a separate bowl and add milk and oil. Gently whisk together with a hand whisk, taking care not to incorporate too much air into the mixture.

Pour egg mixture into muffin mixture. Using a wooden spoon, mix until batter just comes together, taking care not to over-mix or muffins will be tough.

Pour a small amount of batter into each muffin hole. Make a small indentation in the batter, then place one soft-boiled egg in each indentation, blunt end down. Fill muffin holes with rest of batter, making sure each egg is completely encased in batter. Sprinkle muffin tops with grated cheese and place three or four slices of tomato in the centre of each muffin.

Bake in preheated oven for 30–35 minutes, until firm to the touch when pressed with your finger. Remove from oven and allow muffins to settle in the tin (pan) for 10 minutes before turning out and cooling until ready to eat.

Cranberry & Orange Twisted Loaf

Cranberry and orange combined with vanilla white icing – you won't be able to stop at one piece! The secret ingredient in the scone dough is the vanilla extract.

MAKES 2 SMALL TWISTS

FILLING
200g (1¾ cups) dried cranberries, roughly chopped

juice of 3 oranges (150ml/⅔ cup) (or good-quality store-bought orange juice) – zest 2 oranges first and reserve zest for dough

1½ tsp cornflour (cornstarch), mixed to a slurry with 1 tbsp water

DOUGH
400g (2⅔ cups) plain (all-purpose) flour

20g (1¾ tbsp) caster (superfine) sugar

good pinch of salt

25g (1 heaping tbsp) baking powder

zest of 2 oranges

70g (¼ cup) butter, softened

1 egg

1 tsp vanilla extract

200ml (scant 1 cup) milk

1 egg whisked with 1 tbsp water, for egg wash

additional flour for dusting

Vanilla White Icing (page 191)

Prepare filling a day in advance. Place cranberries and juice in a saucepan and bring to the boil. Reduce heat to low, add the cornflour (cornstarch) slurry and cook for 3–4 minutes, stirring occasionally, until thick. The cranberries should soften and swell during cooking. Allow mixture to cool. Tip mixture out onto a chopping (cutting) board and chop with a large chef's knife to give a thick, spreadable paste. Set aside.

The next day, sift flour, sugar, salt and baking powder into a large mixing bowl. Stir in orange zest. Add softened butter and rub in using your fingertips and thumbs until mixture resembles breadcrumbs. Whisk egg, vanilla and milk together in a bowl and pour into dry ingredients. Using a wooden spoon, mix together to form a soft dough.

Tip dough onto a floured work surface and knead for 10–20 seconds. Take care not to over-knead or the dough will become too elastic. Cut dough into two equal pieces and shape into squares. Using a rolling pin on a floured work surface, roll out each dough piece to a 25cm (10in) square.

Divide filling in half. Using a palette knife, spread filling evenly on each dough sheet, leaving about 1cm (½in) free along one edge. Brush egg wash along that edge. Working towards the edge painted with egg wash, firmly and tightly roll up each dough sheet to achieve a Swiss (jelly) roll or log shape. Using a large chef's knife or dough scraper, make a single cut lengthways right through the middle of each log. For each log, take one strand in each hand, with the cut side of each strand facing upwards. Beginning at one end, twist strands around each other down the length of the strands. Press the ends firmly together so they do not unwind during baking.

Place twists on a baking tray (cookie sheet) lined with baking (parchment) paper, keeping them well apart so they don't join together during baking. Brush with egg wash and leave to rest for 10 minutes.

Bake twists in a preheated 210°C/410°F/Gas 6½ oven for 25–30 minutes. Turn tray (sheet) halfway through baking time to ensure an even colour. While loaves are baking, make icing. Cover and set aside.

Remove twists from oven and leave to cool slightly. While they are still warm, gently heat icing in a microwave and use a pastry brush to brush it over the twists. Leave to cool completely before eating.

Hand-dropped Sultana & Raspberry Scones

These scones are very buttery, full of plump sultanas with a nice drop of raspberry jam. They remind me very much of traditional rock cakes made with currants. They look good and are a delight to eat. The secret is to really cream the butter and sugar together until fluffy – this makes it much easier to scoop the batter out with your hands. If you don't like using your hands, use a large serving spoon instead.

MAKES 12–15 SCONES

440g (3 cups) plain (all-purpose) flour

10g (2 tsp) baking powder

¼ tsp bicarbonate of soda (baking soda)

5g (1 tsp) salt

250g (1 cup) butter, softened

110g (½ cup) caster (superfine) sugar

1 small egg

125ml (½ cup) whole milk

1 tsp vanilla extract

250g (1½ cups) sultanas (golden raisins), soaked overnight in 50ml (scant ¼ cup) hot water

1 egg whisked with 1 tbsp water, for egg wash

100g (3½oz) nibbed sugar or coffee sugar crystals, for topping

Homemade Raspberry Jam (page 193) – or good-quality store-bought jam

In a bowl, sift together flour, baking powder, bicarbonate of soda (baking soda) and salt, and set aside.

Place softened butter and caster (superfine) sugar in an electric mixer bowl. Using the beater attachment, beat until really light and creamy. Mix egg, milk and vanilla in a jug (pitcher) and add to the creamed mixture, then add the sifted dry ingredients. Mix for 1 minute on slow speed, then 30 seconds on medium speed. Add sultanas (golden raisins) and blend on low speed until they are evenly mixed in. Scrape down sides of bowl and beater, and remove bowl from mixer.

Line two baking trays (cookie sheets) with baking (parchment) paper. Using a cupped hand, scoop up approximately 100g (3½oz) of batter (weigh the first one to give you an idea of the size) and drop it onto the prepared tray (sheet), leaving at least 3cm (1¼in) between each scone. Repeat until all batter is used up. Brush egg wash over the tops of the scones, then sprinkle evenly with nibbed sugar or coffee sugar crystals.

Stir raspberry jam a little to make it smooth. Place jam into a piping (pastry) bag with a 5mm (¼in) plain nozzle (tip). Plant the nozzle (tip) into the top and centre of each scone. Squeeze the piping (pastry) bag to inject a good couple of teaspoons of jam inside, then withdraw nozzle (tip) slowly until a little jam oozes out onto the top of the scone.

Bake in a preheated 210°C/410°F/Gas 6½ oven for 20–25 minutes. Rotate trays (sheets) halfway through for an even baked colour. Cool on the trays (sheets) for 5 minutes, then place scones on a wire rack to cool completely.

Festive Breads

Panettone

There is a romantic history to this yeasted sweet bread. A young baker called Toni baked this for a wealthy orange farmer, who liked it so much he gave Toni permission to marry his daughter. The dome shape represents churches of that era. This specialty bread is enjoyed at Christmas time. Make it at least 4 weeks in advance, as it improves with age. You will need two non-stick 15cm-(6in-)diameter panettone moulds (available from specialty cookware stores).

MAKES 2 LARGE (15CM/6IN) PANETTONE

SPONGE DOUGH FERMENT

185g (scant 1¼ cups) strong bread flour

2g (scant 1 tsp) instant dry yeast

115ml (½ cup) water, at blood temperature

SOAKED FRUIT

180g (1 cup) sultanas (golden raisins) or raisins

40ml (8tsp) rum

100g (3½oz) mixed peel

DOUGH

500g (3 cups) strong bread flour

10g (2 tsp) salt

115g (½ cup) sugar

5g (1¼ tsp) instant dry yeast

zest of 2 lemons or oranges

1 quantity of Sponge Dough Ferment (from the day before)

1½ tsp pure vanilla extract with seeds

1½ tsp orange blossom water

140g (5oz) egg yolks (approx. 7 eggs)

120ml (½ cup) water

115g (½ cup) butter, softened

1 quantity of Soaked Fruit (from the day before)

100g (scant ½ cup) butter, melted, for brushing on top of baked loaves

Begin sponge dough ferment a day in advance. Mix all ingredients in a bowl. Tip onto a work surface and knead for approximately 5 minutes to form a dough. Place in a bowl, cover with clingfilm (plastic wrap) and leave at room temperature for a minimum of 8 hours, preferably overnight.

To prepare the fruit, place sultanas (golden raisins) or raisins in a bowl, add rum and toss to coat. Cover and soak overnight. Add mixed peel before using.

The next day, place dry ingredients, zest, sponge dough ferment, vanilla and orange blossom water in a large mixing bowl. Mix to combine. Add egg yolks and water. Using a wooden spoon, combine to form a dough.

Tip dough out onto a lightly floured work surface and knead for approximately 5 minutes. The dough will be firm at this stage. Gradually add softened butter over five additions, while still kneading. This process will take some time; the dough will be sticky at first. Knead for 10–15 minutes, resting dough for 1 minute every 2–3 minutes, until it is very smooth, elastic, soft and shiny. Add soaked fruit and peel. Carefully knead into dough until it becomes soft and smooth again and all the fruit is evenly incorporated.

Place dough in a lightly oiled large bowl, cover with clingfilm (plastic wrap) and leave in a warm place for 45 minutes. Knock back dough by folding it onto itself a few times. Cover and leave to rest for a further 30 minutes.

Tip dough out onto a floured work surface and divide into two 800g (1¾lb) pieces. Mould into large boules (page 35). Place boules in two non-stick panettone moulds. Place moulds on a baking tray (cookie sheet) and cover with clingfilm (plastic wrap). Leave to rise for 3–4 hours.

Carefully cut a cross in the top of each fully risen panettone with a sharp knife or razor blade (see image on previous page). Place loaves on tray (sheet) in a preheated 170°C/340°F/Gas 3 oven and bake for 1 hour, until the sides of the panettone feel firm and the tops are golden brown. Remove from oven and immediately brush each loaf with the melted butter. Leave to cool.

My Ultimate Hot Cross Buns

These are so good you'll be making them all the time, not just at Easter – and you'll never buy store-bought hot cross buns again. The spice mixture given in this recipe is enough for two batches – make up and store in an airtight container until required.

MAKES 12 HOT CROSS BUNS

PREPARED FRUIT

175g (1 cup) sultanas (golden raisins)
175g (generous 1 cup) currants
30ml (2 tbsp) rum

DOUGH

500g (3 cups) strong bread flour
15g (½oz) Hot Cross Bun Spice Mixture (page 191)
10g (2 tsp) salt
50g (4 tbsp) butter, softened
50g (¼ cup) sugar
zest of 1 orange
10g (2½ tsp) instant dry yeast
1 egg
350ml (1½ cups) water

additional flour for dusting
Sugar Glaze (page 191)

CROSS MIXTURE

75g (½ cup) plain (all-purpose) flour
25ml (5 tsp) vegetable oil (e.g. rapeseed, canola or sunflower)
75ml (5 tbsp) water

Prepare fruit a day in advance. Place sultanas (golden raisins), currants and rum in a bowl and toss to coat. Cover with clingfilm (plastic wrap) and leave in a warm place overnight.

The next day, place dough ingredients in a large mixing bowl. Using a wooden spoon, combine the ingredients to form a dough mass. Tip dough out onto a lightly floured work surface and knead for 10–15 minutes, resting for 30 seconds every 2–3 minutes, until dough is smooth and elastic. This will take a while; the dough will be sticky to the touch at first, but don't be tempted to add excessive amounts of flour during the kneading process. Add prepared fruit and continue to knead very gently until incorporated into the dough.

Lightly oil a bowl large enough to allow dough to double in bulk. Put dough in bowl and cover with clingfilm (plastic wrap). Leave in a warmish place (23–25°C/73–77°F) for 45–60 minutes. Gently knock back dough in the bowl by folding it back onto itself: it will deflate slightly, but will develop more strength. Cover again with plastic and leave for 30 minutes.

Line a baking tray (cookie sheet) with baking (parchment) paper. Tip dough out onto a lightly floured work surface. Divide into 12 equal pieces, approximately 100g (3½oz) each. Roll each dough piece into a small ball or bun shape (see page 39). Place buns approximately 2cm (¾in) apart on the tray (sheet) so that they join together while proving. Cover with plastic wrap and leave to prove for 45–60 minutes, until buns have almost doubled in size.

Make the cross mixture by placing flour and oil in a bowl. Using a whisk, mix while slowly adding water to form a smooth, lump-free paste. Put paste into a piping (pastry) bag fitted with a 3mm (⅛in) plain nozzle (tip) (or put into a large, strong plastic bag and snip off one corner to make a piping (pastry) bag). Pipe crosses onto the buns.

Place buns on tray (sheet) in a preheated 190°C/375°F/Gas 5 oven and bake for 20–25 minutes or until golden brown. Meanwhile, prepare sugar glaze. Remove buns from oven and brush with sugar glaze. Allow to cool slightly before cutting in half and spreading with butter.

Celebration Loaf

This 'larger than life' loaf is a celebration loaf for that special occasion – or just to impress! Once baked, it gives off a distinctive nutty Chardonnay aroma – from the wine and the wholemeal and rye flours. Its firm and irregular crumb is superb eaten with any meal. Oh, and when lightly toasted it's amazing. It's worth all the effort, trust me!

MAKES 1 LARGE LOAF

SPONGE DOUGH FERMENT

100g (scant ⅔ cup) strong bread flour

good pinch of salt

1g (½ tsp) instant dry yeast

60ml (¼ cup) warm water

DOUGH

400g (scant 2½ cups) strong flour

50g (⅓ cup) wholemeal or whole wheat flour

50g (½ cup) rye flour

1 quantity of Sponge Dough Ferment (from the day before)

10g (2 tsp) salt

5g (1¼ tsp) instant dry yeast

360ml (1½ cups) Chardonnay (or water), tepid

DECORATING THE LOAF

1 quantity of Decorating Dough (page 193), made a day in advance

instant coffee

1 egg whisked with 1 tbsp water, for egg wash

Begin the sponge dough ferment a day in advance. Place all ingredients in a bowl and combine to form a dough. Place on a floured work surface and knead for 8–10 minutes until fully developed. Place in a lightly oiled container, cover with clingfilm (plastic wrap) and leave overnight (12–16 hours) to ferment.

The next day, place all dough ingredients in a large mixing bowl and, using a wooden spoon, combine to form a dough. Tip dough out onto a lightly floured work surface and knead for 10–15 minutes, resting it for 1 minute every 2–3 minutes, until smooth and elastic. Check dough throughout kneading for stickiness; add more water or flour if necessary to achieve a soft, not too firm dough. Place dough in a lightly oiled bowl, cover with clingfilm (plastic wrap) and leave in a warm place for approximately 45 minutes, until dough is gassy and full of life. Gently knock back dough by folding it back onto itself several times. Cover again and leave for a further 45 minutes.

Tip dough out onto a lightly floured work surface. Gently mould dough into a round ball shape by cupping your hands around it and moving them in a circular motion, pulling the skin tight over the dough. Don't overdo this, or the skin will rip and will spoil the appearance of the finished product. The final shape will look like a smooth ball, but with a rough, scrunched-up bottom.

Place the moulded loaf seam-side down onto a baking tray (cookie sheet) lined with baking (parchment) paper. Dust loaf with flour and loosely cover with clingfilm (plastic wrap). Leave to prove for approximately 1½ hours in a warm, draught-free place.

Using a sharp knife or razor blade, gently cut a shallow ring around the loaf, about a quarter of the way up from the bottom. This allows the loaf to expand and split around the bottom rather than at the top, where the decoration will be sitting.

Recipe continued overleaf

DECORATING THE LOAF

Roll out decorating dough and cut 6–8 wheat spears (3–4 with ears of wheat at the end, and the rest just long stalks – see photo). Snip the ends of the ears of wheat many times to represent grains of wheat. Roll out more dough into a large flat plaque that will sit across the loaf. Using small pieces of rolled-out decorating dough, form the letters of the person's name. Brush the back of each letter with water and place on the plaque to stick. Mix a small amount of instant coffee with a little water and paint the letters a brown colour with this so they stand out.

Using a pastry brush and water, gently brush the place on the top of the loaf where you want to place individual wheat spears. Place on the wheat spears, then gently brush the surface of the loaf with water and stick the plaque onto the loaf over the spears. Brush all the decorating dough with egg wash for extra shine and a golden brown colour.

Place loaf in a preheated 230°C/450°F/Gas 8 oven, create steam in the oven (page 44) and quickly close the oven door. Bake for 20 minutes, then lower oven temperature to 200°C/400°F/Gas 6 and bake for a further 20–25 minutes, until bottom of loaf sounds hollow when tapped with your knuckles. Remove loaf from oven and cool on a wire rack.

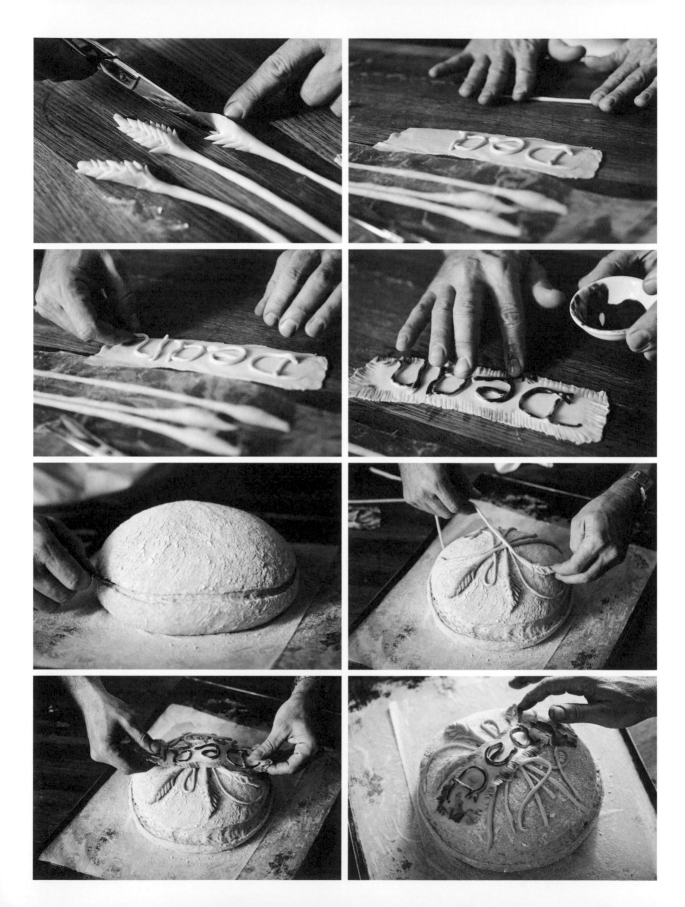

Swedish Christmas Rye Crackers

Imagine a cold winter's night and an antipasto plate of chargrilled vegetables, cold cuts of meat and pâté and these wonderful crackers – and, of course, a lovely full-bodied Pinot Noir. The secret to these crackers is the ground aniseed or fennel. These crackers may be stored in an airtight container for up to 2 weeks.

MAKES 10 LARGE CRACKERS

300g (scant 2 cups) strong bread flour

200g (2 cups) coarsely ground rye flour (stoneground is best)

10g (2 tsp) salt

10g (2 tsp) honey

15g (5 tsp) instant dry yeast

100ml (scant ½ cup) olive oil

2 tsp ground aniseed or ground fennel seeds

300ml (1¼ cups) water

30g (scant ¼ cup) sunflower seeds

30g (¼ cup) pumpkin seeds

25g (2½ tbsp) linseeds (flaxseeds)

25g (2¾ tbsp) sesame seeds

additional rye flour for dusting

Place all ingredients except the seeds in a large mixing bowl and, using a wooden spoon, combine to form a dough. Tip dough out onto a lightly floured work surface and knead for around 15 minutes, resting for 30 seconds every 2–3 minutes, until dough is smooth and elastic. Add seeds and knead until well combined. Place dough in a lightly oiled bowl and cover with clingfilm (plastic wrap). Leave in a warm place for 30 minutes.

Tip dough onto a work surface lightly sprinkled with rye flour. Cut dough into 10 equal pieces, approximately 100g (3½oz) each. Very gently mould each piece into a small, round ball shape. Leave dough pieces on floured work surface, cover with clingfilm (plastic wrap) and rest for 5 minutes. Line two baking trays (cookie sheets) with baking (parchment) paper.

Flatten each ball with the palm of your hand. Using a rolling pin, roll out each dough piece to a 20cm-(8in-)diameter circle. Use plenty of rye flour on top and bottom of dough pieces – this prevents dough from sticking to the work surface, and it gives a rustic look to the baked crackers. Using a 3cm (1¼in) round cutter, cut a hole in the middle of each disc. Reserve the cut-out holes and roll into another disc when finished. Using the end of a pencil or a chopstick, poke holes evenly over each disc. (Alternatively, roll dough out to a 3mm-(⅛in-) thick rectangle, poke holes as described above, cut into squares or rectangles, then proceed as below.)

Place dough pieces on trays (sheets), cover with plastic and leave in a warm place for 30 minutes, until dough has risen and is a little puffy.

Place both trays in a preheated 180°C/350°F/Gas 4 oven and bake for 30 minutes. Reduce heat to 160°C/325°F/Gas 3 and bake for a further 15–20 minutes. The aim is to dry out the crackers; you can open the oven door a little to allow some of the moisture to escape. Remove trays (sheets) from oven and place crackers on a wire rack to cool.

Dresden Christmas Stollen

The tradition of baking Dresden Stollen goes back to the fifteenth century. It was originally made without butter or milk, and was a rather dull pastry, until Lord Ernst of Saxony and his brother Albrecht appealed to the Pope to rescind the 'butter ban' so these important ingredients could be included. Make Stollen at least a month in advance to allow the flavour to mature. Great served with coffee or tea at Christmastime.

MAKES 2 STOLLEN

PREPARED FRUIT

120g (scant ¾ cup) sultanas (golden raisins)

120g (scant 1 cup) currants or raisins

50ml (scant ¼ cup) rum

50g (½ cup) flaked (slivered) almonds, lightly roasted in 170°C/340°F/Gas 3 oven until amber

50g (2oz) mixed peel

STARTER DOUGH

100ml (scant ½ cup) milk, at room temperature

7g (2½ tsp) instant dry yeast

140g (scant 1 cup) strong bread flour

STOLLEN DOUGH

1 quantity of Starter Dough

170g (1 cup) strong bread flour

2 good pinches of salt

35g (2 heaping tbsp) sugar

¼ tsp ground nutmeg

¼ tsp ground cardamom

1 tsp pure vanilla extract with seeds

80ml (⅓ cup) milk

120g (½ cup) butter, softened, divided into 3 x 40g (scant ¼ cup) portions

FILLING AND TOPPING

200g (7oz) good-quality marzipan, rolled into 2 x 20cm (8in) logs

150g (⅔ cup) unsalted butter

70g (¾ cup) icing (confectioners') sugar, plus extra for dusting

150g (¾ cup) caster (superfine) sugar

Prepare fruit a day in advance. Place sultanas (golden raisins), currants or raisins and rum in a bowl and toss to coat evenly. Cover with clingfilm (plastic wrap) and leave in a warm place overnight.

The next day, add the almonds and mixed peel to the prepared fruit.

Prepare starter dough by placing all ingredients in a large mixing bowl and, using a wooden spoon, combining to form a dough. Tip dough out onto work surface and knead for 10 minutes until dough is smooth and silky. Place in a lightly oiled bowl, cover with clingfilm (plastic wrap) and leave to ferment in a warm place for 30 minutes.

Place starter dough, flour, salt, sugar, spices, vanilla, milk and the first 40g (scant ¼ cup) portion of butter in a large mixing bowl. Using your hand, combine to form a dough mass. Tip dough out onto a lightly floured work surface and knead for approximately 5 minutes. Add second 40g (scant ¼ cup) butter and continue to knead until it is well mixed in. Add final 40g (scant ¼ cup) butter and knead until dough is smooth and elastic. This will take a while, as the dough will be sticky to the touch at first. Over three additions, add the rum-soaked fruit, peel and almonds and continue to knead very gently until they are incorporated into the dough. Take your time.

Lightly oil a bowl large enough to allow dough to double in bulk. Put dough in bowl and cover with clingfilm (plastic wrap). Leave in a warm place for 45 minutes.

Line a baking tray (cookie sheet) with baking (parchment) paper. Tip dough onto a lightly floured work surface. Divide into two equal pieces, approximately 500g (1lb 2oz) each. Form each piece into an oblong approximately 22cm x 20cm (8½in x 8in), and flatten it with the palm of your hand. Place one of the marzipan rolls slightly off-centre on each dough piece and fold over so marzipan is enclosed in dough. Using the handles of two wooden spoons, press dough firmly down on either side of the dough-covered marzipan sausage to create the typical Stollen shape (see photo). Place on prepared baking tray (cookie sheet), cover with clingfilm (plastic wrap) and leave to rest for 15 minutes.

Bake Stollen in a preheated 180°C/350°F/Gas 4 oven for 40–45 minutes or until golden brown. Remove from oven and cool for 20 minutes on a wire rack. When Stollen are cool, make the topping. Place butter in a saucepan and melt over a low heat. Add icing (confectioners') sugar and whisk until smooth. Bring to the boil, then remove from heat.

Using a pastry brush, generously brush each Stollen with the melted butter and sugar mix to coat completely, then place on a wire rack to drain for 1 hour. Repeat process three more times, resting for 2–3 minutes between each brushing to allow the butter and sugar mixture to soak in. Cover Stollen in a thick layer of caster (superfine) sugar. Rest Stollen overnight in a covered container or on a tray covered with clingfilm (plastic wrap).

The next day, using a sieve (strainer), heavily dust Stollen with icing (confectioners') sugar. Wrap Stollen individually in cellophane or clingfilm (plastic wrap) and store for a minimum of 4 weeks before cutting and eating.

Panforte

Christmas in Italy would not be complete without this wonderful spiced, peppery candied fruit and nut confectionery. Pan means bread and forte means strong, so in effect it's a strong bread. Panforte is great with a rich red wine or port, or enjoy it with an espresso at the end of a fantastic meal.

MAKES 1 x 20CM (8IN) ROUND CAKE

115g (¾ cup) hazelnuts, skinned

115g (¾ cup) whole almonds, skinned

40g (1½oz) each: glacé (candied) pineapple, dried apricots, crystallised ginger and dried figs, cut into 5mm (¼in) pieces

130g (4½oz) mixed (lemon and orange) peel, chopped

1 tsp ground Chinese five spice

½ tsp each: ground coriander, cloves, nutmeg

¼ tsp white pepper

100g (⅔ cup) plain (all-purpose) flour

150g (¾ cup) sugar

125g (⅓ cup) honey

30g (2 tbsp) butter

To roast hazelnuts and almonds, preheat oven to 180°C/350°F/Gas 4. Place nuts on an oven tray and put into preheated oven for 10–15 minutes until nuts turn a pale amber colour. Remove from oven and cool, then coarsely chop into pieces.

Lower oven temperature to 170°C/340°F/Gas 3. Line bottom and sides of a 20cm (8in) spring-form cake tin (pan) with baking (parchment) paper.

Mix chopped nuts, fruits, peel, spices and flour thoroughly in a large bowl.

Place sugar, honey and butter in a heavy-bottomed saucepan and cook over a medium heat until mixture reaches 116°C (241°F) on a candy thermometer ('soft ball' stage – test by dropping some mixture from a spoon into a jug (pitcher) of cold water, then rubbing it together between your thumb and forefinger; it should form a soft ball). Take care, as sugar cooks quickly. Remove from heat and immediately pour hot sugar syrup onto flour and nut mixture and stir quickly using a wooden spoon until well combined. The mixture will cool and become very stiff, so it's important to work very quickly at this stage.

Place mixture into prepared cake tin (pan). Using your knuckles dipped in cold water, gently press the mixture evenly into the tin (pan) until level and smooth – again working quickly to avoid the mixture becoming too stiff on cooling.

Place tin (pan) immediately in preheated oven and bake for 30–40 minutes, until the outside edges begin to firm up. The panforte won't colour very much or seem very firm directly after baking, but it will harden up as it cools.

Cool panforte in the tin (pan) until firm, then remove from tin (pan) and peel off the baking (parchment) paper. Cool completely and store in an airtight container for up to 3 months.

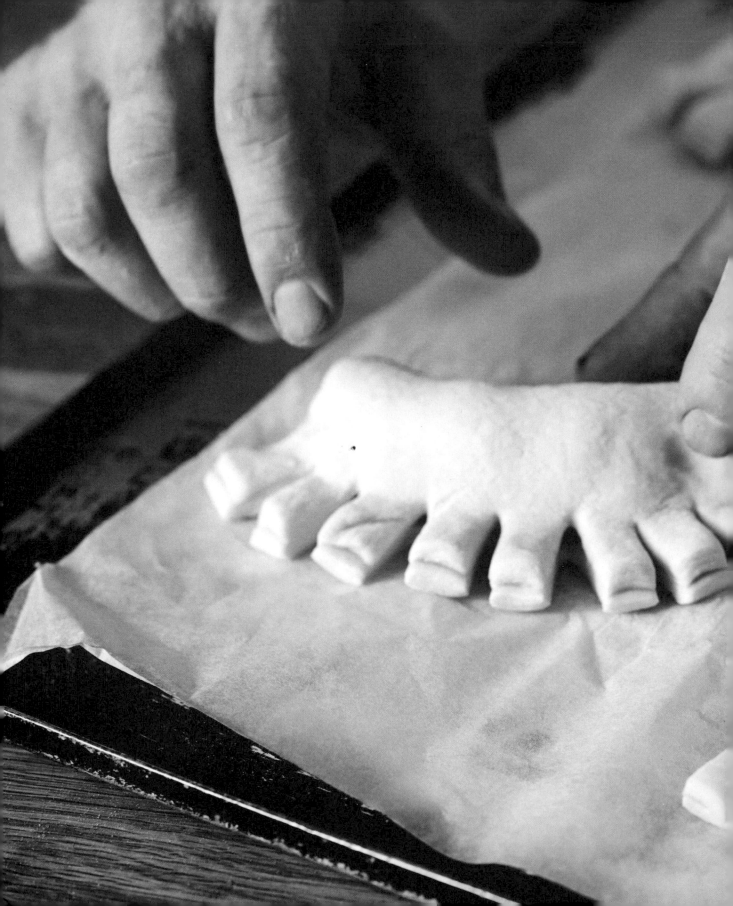

Not Quite Bread

Wholemeal Spicy Lavash-style Crackers

Lavash crackers have a spicy Asian influence to them, and are just divine with any pâté or hummus. Once baked and crisp, they can be stored in an airtight container for up to 1 month – not that they will last that long!

MAKES 40 TRIANGULAR CRACKERS

SPICE MIXTURE
1 tsp anise seeds
2 tsp sesame seeds
½ tsp nigella seeds (or use onion seeds)
½ tsp sea-salt flakes
¼ tsp hot chilli powder

DOUGH
100g (⅔ cup) plain (all-purpose) flour
100g (⅔ cup) wholemeal or whole wheat flour
½ tsp salt
1½ tsp olive oil
1 tsp red chilli (pepper) flakes
120ml (½ cup) (approx.) warm water

To make spice mixture, bruise anise seeds slightly by grinding in a mortar and pestle, or using a rolling pin on a chopping (cutting) board. Stir all spice ingredients together in a small bowl and set aside.

Place flours, salt, oil and chilli (pepper) flakes in a medium bowl. Add water slowly, stirring with a wooden spoon, until you achieve a firm dough. If dough is too dry, add an extra 1–2 tablespoons of water; if it is too sticky, add 2–3 tablespoons of flour.

Tip dough ball out onto a work surface and knead by hand for 5 minutes, resting dough for 1 minute every 2–3 minutes, until it is firm but smooth. Place in a lightly floured bowl, cover with clingfilm (plastic wrap) and leave to rest for 30 minutes.

Tip dough out onto a lightly floured work surface and cut into five equal pieces. Mould each dough piece into a ball, cover with clingfilm (plastic wrap) and leave to rest again for 20 minutes.

Line a baking tray (cookie sheet) with baking (parchment) paper. On a lightly floured work surface, roll each dough ball to a thin 20cm-(8in-) diameter circle and place it on the lined baking tray (cookie sheet). Lightly brush dough circles with water and sprinkle about ½ teaspoon of the spice mixture over each. Wipe the blade of a large sharp knife or pizza cutter with olive oil, then cut each circle into eight equal pieces (do not separate them).

Place tray in a preheated 250°C/500°F/Gas 10 oven and bake for 5–8 minutes, until the crackers are golden brown. Take care during the baking, as they are thin and will colour up very quickly. Remove crackers from the tray (sheet) and break them into wedges.

Cool the baking tray (cookie sheet) and repeat the rolling, seasoning, cutting and baking process for the remaining dough balls.

Pain d'épices

Some people call this French gingerbread loaf, but to me it's far more complex than that and contains a completely different mixture of spices, in particular aniseed. Even if you think you don't like aniseed, try this loaf – it's amazing. And it's even better toasted or grilled (broiled) for a minute or two, and served spread with butter.

MAKES 1 x 23CM (9IN) LOAF

450g (3 cups) plain (all-purpose) flour
60g (⅔ cup) dark rye flour
2½ tsp bicarbonate of soda (baking soda)
1½ tsp Chinese five spice
1½ tsp ground ginger
¼ tsp ground cloves
½ tsp salt
¼ tsp freshly grated nutmeg
¼ tsp freshly ground black pepper
½ tsp anise seeds
55g (¼ cup) butter, at room temperature
1 large egg, at room temperature
340g (1 cup) honey
1 tbsp finely grated orange zest
240ml (1 cup) water

Preheat oven to 180°C/350°F/Gas 4. Lightly brush a 23cm (9in) loaf tin (pan) with melted butter, dust it with flour, then tap out any excess flour.

In a bowl, sift together flours, bicarbonate of soda (baking soda), ground spices and salt. Add grated nutmeg and ground pepper, and sprinkle in anise seeds.

In a separate large bowl, using a hand whisk, mix together butter, egg, honey and orange zest until well combined. Add the water. Using a spatula, add the dry ingredients in three additions, scraping the sides of the bowl to make sure everything gets mixed in evenly.

Pour the batter into the prepared loaf tin (pan). Bake in preheated oven for 1 hour, or until the top is quite dark and a skewer inserted into the centre comes out clean. Cool for 10 minutes, then tip out and place on a wire rack to cool completely before slicing.

Danish Smørrebrød

Danish Smørrebrød are lovely little open sandwiches. Serve them with a little salad on the side and a glass of crisp white wine. These are definitely not picnic or finger-food – they are best eaten with a knife and fork. I have not given you a precise recipe, just some thoughts to excite your taste buds!

BREAD

Use a Danish Rugbrød (page 101) or a similar heavy bread, cut into 1cm (½in) slices. It is important to choose a fairly close-textured bread – if you use an open holey sourdough, the fillings will fall through.

Lightly toast one side of each slice, if you like, for extra crunchiness.

TOPPING SUGGESTIONS

+ Egg mayonnaise topped with sliced fresh salmon, radish, cucumber and capers

+ Tuna mayonnaise topped with shaved Parmesan, sweetcorn, sundried tomatoes and chopped chives

+ Mozzarella, tomato, basil and extra virgin olive oil

+ Parma-(prosciutto-)style ham with ricotta cheese and rocket (arugula) and oven-roasted tomatoes with olive oil and lemon dressing

+ Pâté foie gras with bean shoots, olive oil, capers and finely sliced red onion

+ Sundried tomatoes, sautéed mushrooms, green stuffed olives, roasted (bell) pepper and shaved Parmesan

Banana Bread

You can't go past a good homemade banana bread. One slice after another and before you know it you have eaten a whole loaf. Make sure you use really ripe bananas, as they bring about a deep, sweet banana flavour. Often I spread a cream cheese icing (frosting) on top, finished with toasted chopped walnuts – but it wouldn't be a bread then, would it!

MAKES 1 x 23CM (9IN) LOAF

220g (1½ cups) self-raising flour
¼ tsp bicarbonate of soda (baking soda)
¼ tsp ground cinnamon
¼ tsp salt
80g (scant ½ cup) sugar
45g (¼ cup) brown sugar
2 eggs
60ml (¼ cup) milk
1 tsp vanilla extract
75g (5 tbsp) melted butter or vegetable oil
200g (7oz) mashed ripe banana
20–30g (¼–⅓ cup) rolled oats, for topping

Preheat oven to 180°C/350°F/Gas 4. Lightly brush a 23cm (9in) loaf tin (pan) with melted butter.

In a large bowl, sift together self-raising flour, bicarbonate of soda (baking soda), cinnamon and salt.

In a separate bowl, using a hand whisk, mix together sugars, eggs, milk, vanilla and butter or oil, then stir in the mashed banana until well combined.

Add the wet ingredients to the dry ingredients and quickly stir, using a spatula, until just combined.

Pour batter into the prepared loaf tin (pan) and sprinkle the top evenly with rolled oats. Bake in preheated oven for 40–45 minutes, or until a skewer inserted into the centre of the loaf comes out clean. Cool in the tin (pan) for 10 minutes, then tip loaf out onto a wire rack to cool completely before slicing.

Panzanella Bread Salad

Use a firm bread and make sure it's at least one or two days old – if the bread is too fresh, it will disintegrate as soon as the liquids are added. This makes a great barbecue salad to serve with a juicy beef steak.

SERVES 6–8

1 red (bell) pepper

1 yellow (bell) pepper

8 tomatoes

½–¾ red onion

1 spring onion (scallion)

300–400g (11–14oz) day-old crusty country bread (e.g. Pain au Levain, page 58)

4 tbsp white wine vinegar

1 cucumber

60–125ml (¼–½ cup) extra virgin olive oil

2 small cloves garlic, crushed

bunch of fresh basil, torn into small pieces

Blacken (bell) peppers over a gas hob (stove) or using a kitchen blowtorch, then put in a plastic bag and leave to sweat for 20 minutes.

Cut tomatoes into large chunks. Slice red onion and chop spring onion (scallion) into 1cm (½in) pieces. Place tomatoes and onions in a bowl, season with a few good pinches of salt and set aside to macerate.

Cut bread into chunks of similar size to the tomatoes. Put in a large mixing bowl, add vinegar and toss together. Set aside.

Scrape as much black skin off the peppers as you can, remove the seeds and core, and cut peppers into long strips. Cut cucumber into large chunks of a similar size to the tomatoes and bread.

Whisk olive oil and crushed garlic together, and season with salt and pepper.

Place all the prepared vegetables in the bowl with the bread. Pour the olive oil mixture over, add basil, toss all the ingredients together and let marinate, covered, for at least 30 minutes and up to 1 hour.

Serve at room temperature.

Danish Pastries

Danish pastries were introduced to Denmark in 1850. When bakers in Denmark went on strike over wages, bakery owners hired foreign bakers, especially from Austria. The Austrian bakers were unfamiliar with Danish baking methods, so they baked classic pastries from Austria. When the strike ended there was public demand for these Austrian pastries, which became known as 'Danish pastries'.

MAKES APPROXIMATELY 24 DANISH PASTRIES

PASTRY DOUGH
750g (4½ cups) strong bread flour

15g (1 tbsp) salt

75g (generous ⅓ cup) caster (superfine) sugar

20g (2 heaping tbsp) instant dry yeast

2 eggs

400ml (1¾ cups) (approx.) whole milk, chilled

300g (1¼ cups) butter for rolling, cold (but not too hard)

CROWNS
1 quantity of Crème Pâtissière (page 192)

16–20 canned apricot halves or any other canned fruits (drained from their juices)

SNAILS
10g (3 tsp) ground cinnamon

100g (½ cup) granulated sugar

BEAR CLAWS
1 quantity of Almond Cream (page 192)

450g (1lb) canned sour cherries, drained

70g (¾ cup) flaked (slivered) almonds

TOPPINGS
1 egg whisked with 50ml water, for egg wash

Apricot Glaze (page 191)

White Icing (page 191) (optional)

icing (confectioners') sugar, for dusting (optional)

Prepare the dough a day in advance. Place the flour, salt, sugar, yeast, eggs and milk in a mixing bowl and, using your hands, combine to form a dough mass. Tip dough out onto a lightly floured surface and knead for 10–15 minutes, resting for 30 seconds every 2–3 minutes, until smooth and elastic. The dough will be very firm and 'tight'. Don't add more liquid at this stage, as the dough will become too soft later. Place dough in a lightly oiled large bowl, cover with clingfilm (plastic wrap) and leave in a warm place for 1 hour, until almost doubled in size.

Tip dough onto the work surface and gently deflate it by folding it onto itself three or four times. Return dough to bowl, cover with clingfilm (plastic wrap) and refrigerate overnight.

Knock the butter into a 17cm (6in) square by hitting it with a rolling pin; this will soften the butter. Wrap in clingfilm (plastic wrap) and chill again.

The next day, tip dough out onto a lightly floured work surface and roll out to a 30cm x 30cm x 1cm-(12in x 12in x ½in-)thick square. Make sure the butter is the same consistency as the dough. Place it inside the dough square.

Fold each corner of the dough into the centre to encase the layering butter in an envelope, giving two layers of dough and one layer of butter. Roll out the pastry to a rectangle 1.5cm (⅝in) thick, then mentally divide the rectangle into thirds. Following the diagram below, fold A to C, then fold D to B, to give three layers of pastry – this is called a 'single turn'.

Cover with clingfilm (plastic wrap) and rest for 20 minutes in the refrigerator. Repeat this process (rolling and folding), cover and rest for 20 minutes in the refrigerator.

Repeat the process once again; you should now have given the pastry three single turns. Rest the pastry in the refrigerator for a final 20 minutes, in preparation for final rolling.

Prepare toppings. Line two baking trays (cookie sheets) with baking (parchment) paper.

Remove pastry from refrigerator and tip out onto a floured work surface. Using a rolling pin, roll out to 4–5mm (⅙–¼in) thick, cut into various shapes and add toppings (see next pages).

CROWNS

Cut dough into 11cm (4½in) squares. Fold each corner of a square into the middle to form a pillow (see image 1). Press firmly down in the middle to seal the ends and stop them from popping up during proving and baking. Place crowns on prepared baking tray (cookie sheet). Brush with egg wash (see image 3). Pipe a blob of crème pâtissière in the middle of the pillow (see image 4), then place apricot halves or other fruits into the crème pâtissière filling (see image 5). Prove and bake as instructed on page 153.

SNAILS

Roll dough out to a 3mm (⅛in) rectangle and cut in half vertically so you have two pastry sheets. Sprinkle half of one sheet with cinnamon mixed with sugar (see image 1). Lay the other half on top and give it a gentle roll with a rolling pin. Cut into approximately 2cm-(¾in-)wide strips (see image 3). Using both hands, roll and twist each strip in opposite directions to form a rope (see image 4). Keeping the rope twisted, shape it into a spiral snail shape (see image 5). Tuck the end under the outer coil to stop it from unwinding. Place snails on baking tray (cookie sheet) and brush with egg wash. Prove and bake as instructed on page 153.

BEAR CLAWS

Cut pastry dough into strips at least 11cm (4½in) wide. Half-fill a pastry bag with almond cream and pipe a stripe just off-centre down each strip (see image 1), then place the drained cherries on top of the stripe of almond cream (see image 2). Brush egg wash onto one edge of each strip, then fold strip over filling and press firmly to seal it (see images 3–4). Cut strips into 12cm (5in) pieces, then cut 1cm (½in) slits into the sealed edge to make the 'claws' (see image 5, opposite). Place bear claws on prepared baking tray (cookie sheet), and bend so the claws are spread apart (see image 6). Brush each piece with egg wash and sprinkle sliced or flaked (slivered) almonds over the top (see images 7–8). Prove and bake as instructed opposite.

For all Danish pastries, loosely cover with clingfilm (plastic wrap) and leave to rise for approximately 1 hour. Brush with egg wash again, if needed. Place trays in a preheated 220°C/425°F/Gas 7 oven and bake for at least 20–25 minutes. Swap trays (sheets) around halfway through baking to ensure all pastries are evenly baked and golden brown in colour.

Remove pastries from oven and leave on tray (sheet) to cool for 5 minutes, then transfer to a wire rack. Brush liberally with apricot glaze to give a nice shine. When cool, ice with white icing or dust with icing (confectioners') sugar, if desired.

Nutella Spiced French Toast

French toast is a perfect way to use up any leftover bread. Choose a rich bread such as a brioche rather than a hard, crusty baguette or sourdough: the bread should be tender once it absorbs the sweet custard and is then lightly pan-fried. The Nutella adds to the richness, cut through by the mascarpone and lemon curd. This is real lazy Sunday brunch food at its best.

SERVES 4

1 loaf day-old good-quality bread (e.g. brioche or raisin bread)

1 small jar of Nutella or chocolate & hazelnut spread

4 tbsp butter, for frying

icing (confectioners') sugar, for dusting

250g (1 cup) mascarpone

maple syrup

100g (¼ cup) homemade lemon curd (or good-quality store-bought curd)

250g (9oz) mixed fresh berries

SWEET CUSTARD

3 eggs

200ml (scant 1 cup) milk

70ml (¼ cup) cream

30g (2 tbsp) caster (superfine) sugar

1 tsp vanilla extract

1 tsp Chinese five spice or mixed spice

good pinch of salt

Make the custard by whisking all the ingredients together in a large bowl. Pour into a flat serving dish and set aside.

Cut eight thick slices of bread. Spread a good layer of Nutella on one slice, then place a second slice on top to form a sandwich. Make four sandwiches, and cut each one in half. Dunk each sandwich half in the custard mixture, soaking both sides.

Heat a large, shallow frying pan (skillet) over a medium heat. Add 1 tablespoon of butter and heat until it becomes frothy. Place sandwich halves in pan and cook on both sides until golden brown. Remove from the pan and place in a preheated 100°C/212°F/Gas ¼ oven to keep warm while you finish off the others.

Dust with icing (confectioners') sugar and serve hot with a dollop of mascarpone, maple syrup, a small dollop of lemon curd and fresh berries.

Spiced Chocolate, Cointreau &
Sour Cherry Bread Pudding

Nothing beats a warm bread and butter pudding on a cold winter's night. I have added a twist to this recipe by adding spices, chocolate, Cointreau and sour cherries. Serve with vanilla ice cream – simple!

SERVES 4–6

100g (scant 1 cup) dried sour cherries (or dried cranberries)

75ml (5 tbsp) Cointreau (or other orange liqueur, or rum)

softened butter, for spreading

1 day-old baguette (or other leftover bread), cut into approx. 30 slices

150g (5oz) chocolate, roughly chopped

3 eggs

30g (2 tbsp) caster (superfine) sugar

500ml (2 cups) milk

125ml (½ cup) cream

1 tsp vanilla extract

100g (3½oz) chocolate, roughly chopped

1½ tsp Chinese five spice

50g (¼ cup) sugar, for sprinkling

icing (confectioners') sugar, for dusting

Prepare the cherries (or cranberries) a day in advance by placing them in a small bowl and sprinkling with Cointreau. Heat in the microwave oven for 1 minute on high. Cover with clingfilm (plastic wrap) and leave to soak overnight, tossing occasionally to ensure the cherries absorb all the liqueur. If you don't have a microware, gently heat together in a saucepan to blood-heat.

The next day, butter each slice of bread on one side only. Grease a 1-litre (1-quart) baking dish with butter. Layer the buttered bread buttered-side up in the baking dish, sprinkling the soaked cherries and the first measure of chopped chocolate between each layer. Place the top layer of bread buttered-side up.

Put eggs and sugar in a large bowl and whisk together briefly. Heat milk, cream and vanilla in a saucepan over a medium heat until just boiling. Remove from the heat and add the second measure of chopped chocolate and the Chinese five spice. Leave to stand for 5 minutes, then whisk until the chocolate has completely melted.

Whisk chocolate mixture into the eggs and sugar to create a thin custard. Pour custard over bread slices. Press slices down into the custard to completely submerge them. Sprinkle with sugar and cover the baking dish with greaseproof (wax) paper. Leave to soak for approximately 30 minutes.

Bake for 20 minutes in a preheated 160°C/325°F/Gas 3 oven, still covered with the greaseproof (wax) paper. Remove the paper from the pudding and bake for a further 45–60 minutes, until the custard has just set and the pudding has risen up slightly, and the bread slices have turned crispy around the edges. Allow to cool slightly, then dust with icing (confectioners') sugar and serve with cream or ice cream.

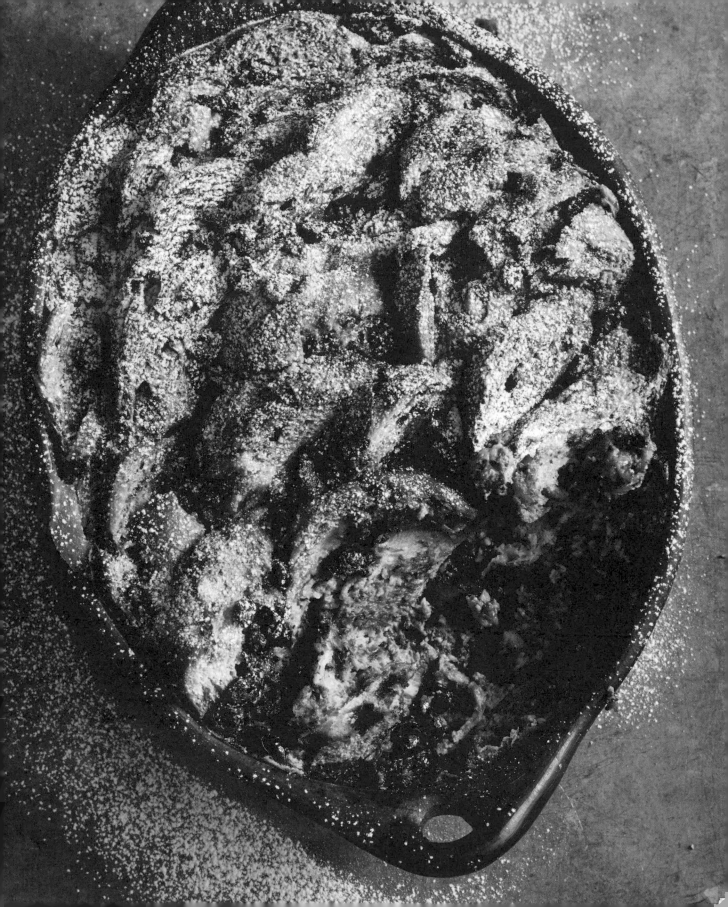

Cinnamon Doughnut Balls

Make plenty of these, as once the kids taste them they will be gone in no time! Fry the doughnuts to a rich golden brown colour and toss them in the cinnamon sugar while they are still hot.

MAKES 20 DOUGHNUT BALLS

DOUGH
500g (3 cups) strong bread flour
10g (2 tsp) salt
60g (⅓ cup) sugar
75g (⅓ cup) butter
10g (3 heaping tsp) instant dry yeast
2 eggs
1 tsp vanilla extract
zest of 1 lemon
210–230ml (scant 1 cup) milk

2 litres (8½ cups) rapeseed (canola) or sunflower oil, for frying

CINNAMON SUGAR
100g (½ cup) sugar mixed with 5–10g (1½–3 tsp) ground cinnamon

Place all dough ingredients in a large mixing bowl and, using a wooden spoon, combine to form a dough mass. Tip dough out onto a lightly floured surface and knead for 10–15 minutes, resting dough for 1 minute every 2–3 minutes, until smooth and elastic. This will take a while; the dough will be sticky to the touch at first, but don't be tempted to add excessive amounts of flour during the kneading process – just persevere with the softness.

Lightly oil a bowl large enough for dough to double in bulk. Put dough in bowl, cover with clingfilm (plastic wrap) and leave in a warmish place (23–25°C/73–77°F) for 30 minutes.

Gently knock back dough in the bowl by gently folding it back onto itself; it will deflate slightly, but will develop more strength. Cover again with clingfilm (plastic wrap) and leave for 30 minutes.

Line a baking tray (cookie sheet) with baking (parchment) paper, lightly sprayed with cooking spray or brushed with vegetable oil.

Tip dough onto a lightly floured work surface and divide into 20 equal pieces, approximately 50g (2oz) each. Roll each dough piece into a small ball.

Place doughnut balls 5cm (2in) apart on prepared baking tray (cookie sheet). Loosely cover with clingfilm (plastic wrap) and leave to rise at room temperature for about 1 hour, until doughnut balls have doubled in size and appear light and full of air.

Heat the oil for about 15 minutes in a large saucepan until it reaches 180°C/350°F. Check the temperature with a candy thermometer and take care not to let the oil heat over 180°C/350°F, as this will result in a doughy, uncooked doughnut. Carefully lift doughnut balls, one at a time, and lower them into the hot oil. Cook 5–7 doughnuts at one time, so that they fry evenly. Fry for 2 minutes on one side, turn them over with a wooden spoon and fry for a further 2 minutes, until golden brown. As they fry, they will increase in size.

Remove doughnuts with a large slotted spoon and drain on kitchen paper (paper towels) for 15 seconds. While the doughnuts are still hot, roll them in cinnamon sugar until evenly coated. They are ready to eat!

Sweet Breads

Apple & Custard Brioche Tarts

These are a cross between a tart and a sweet bread. Using a brioche base gives the tarts a yeasty foundation, and the creamy custard topping adds to the richness and keeps the tarts moist.

MAKES 10 TARTS

BRIOCHE BASE

250g (1½ cups) strong bread flour

5g (1 tsp) salt

25g (2 tbsp) sugar

5g (1¼ tsp) instant dry yeast

30ml (2 tbsp) cold water

3 eggs (150g/5oz when cracked), lightly whisked and chilled

125g (½ cup) butter, softened

Crème Pâtissière (page 192)

1 egg whisked with 1 tbsp water, for egg wash

8 medium Granny Smith apples (or other firm fruit, e.g. peaches, apricots, pears or cherries)

50g (¼ cup) sugar

Apricot Glaze (page 191), optional

Begin brioche base a day in advance. Mix together flour, salt, sugar and yeast in a large mixing bowl. Add water and three-quarters of the whisked egg. Using a wooden spoon, combine to form a dough.

Tip dough out onto a lightly floured work surface and knead for 5 minutes. Gradually add the rest of the egg in small additions while still kneading, until dough starts to become strong, elastic and smooth. Add softened butter in five additions while still kneading. The dough will be sticky at first. Continue kneading for 10–15 minutes, resting for 30 seconds every 3–4 minutes, until dough is very smooth, elastic, soft and shiny. Place in a lightly oiled large bowl, cover with clingfilm (plastic wrap) and leave in a warm place for 1 hour, until it has almost doubled in size.

Tip dough onto the work surface and gently deflate by folding it onto itself three or four times. Return it to the bowl, cover with clingfilm (plastic wrap) and chill overnight (12 hours). This makes it easier to work into the final shape. Make crème pâtissière and keep in the refrigerator.

The next day, line two baking trays (cookie sheets) with baking (parchment) paper and lightly dust a tray with flour. Remove dough from refrigerator and divide into 10 pieces, around 60g (2¼oz) each. Mould into a round ball shape, place on the floured tray and return to the refrigerator for 10 minutes.

Place one dough ball at a time on floured work surface. Using a rolling pin, roll out to a 10cm (4in) disc and place on baking tray. Repeat for all balls. Cover with clingfilm (plastic wrap) and leave for 30 minutes in a warm place to rise.

Brush egg wash on each disc. Put crème pâtissière in a piping (pastry) bag fitted with a 1cm (½in) plain nozzle (tip) and pipe a small spiral of pastry cream on each disc, leaving 1cm (½in) around the edge. Peel, core and slice apple in 1mm (¹⁄₃₂in) slices. Fan slices out in a tight circle on top of crème pâtissière. Sprinkle with sugar.

Bake in a preheated 190–200°C/375–400°F/Gas 5–6 oven for 18–20 minutes, or until the edges of the tarts are light golden brown and the apple slices have started to turn brown around the edges. Remove from oven and brush apricot glaze over apple slices, if desired. Serve cold or warm.

Chocolate Chip Brioche Breakfast Plait

I call this a breakfast plait simply because brioche is a breakfast bread – it's very buttery, yeasty and soft. Serve with your favourite jam. You can substitute the filling with your choice – try a savoury filling such as cheese, bacon and onion. Instead of a plait, you can use a large brioche mould; or roll the dough into small round buns, prove and bake as petites brioches.

MAKES 2 LARGE PLAITED BRIOCHES

BRIOCHE DOUGH
500g (3 cups) strong bread flour

10g (2 tsp) salt

50g (¼ cup) sugar

12g (4 tsp) instant dry yeast

60ml (¼ cup) cold water

6 eggs (300g/11oz when cracked), at room temperature

200g (scant 1 cup) butter, softened

200g (generous 1 cup) chocolate chips, chilled

additional flour for dusting

1 egg mixed with 2 tbsp water, for egg wash

nibbed sugar or crushed sugar cubes, to decorate

Begin the brioche dough a day ahead by mixing flour, salt, sugar and yeast together in a large mixing bowl. Add water and eggs and combine, using a wooden spoon, to form a dough. Tip dough out onto a lightly floured work surface and knead for 5–8 minutes until dough starts to become strong, elastic and smooth.

Add softened butter gradually, in 6–8 additions, while still kneading. The dough will be sticky at first. Knead for 10–15 minutes, resting it for 1 minute every 2–3 minutes, until dough is very smooth, elastic, soft and shiny. Knead in chocolate chips. Place dough in a lightly oiled large bowl, cover with clingfilm (plastic wrap) and leave in a warm place for 1 hour, until it has almost doubled in size.

Uncover dough and tip out onto the work surface. Gently deflate by folding it onto itself three or four times, then return dough to the bowl, cover with clingfilm (plastic wrap) and place in the refrigerator overnight (12 hours). This makes the dough easier to shape.

The next day, line a baking tray (cookie sheet) with baking (parchment) paper. Remove dough from refrigerator and cut into six equal pieces, approximately 220g (7¾oz) each. Roll each piece into a 30cm-(12in-)long rope. Join three dough ropes by pinching together at one end. Plait (braid) them, and squeeze the ropes together at the other end.

Place on prepared baking tray (cookie sheet) with enough space between them to allow brioches to double in size. Cover with clingfilm (plastic wrap) and leave to rise in a warm, draught-free place for 2–2½ hours, until almost doubled in size.

Lightly brush brioches with egg wash and sprinkle with nibbed sugar, then place in a preheated 190°C/375°F/Gas 5 oven. Bake for 20–25 minutes or until golden brown. Remove from oven and cool on a wire rack.

Raspberry-iced Cream Finger Buns

These have to be the ultimate child's dream – a sweet cream finger bun with pink icing. It's an iconic Kiwi bakery product that I grew up with. Yum!

MAKES 12 FINGER BUNS

DOUGH
500g (3 cups) strong bread flour
10g (2 tsp) salt
50g (2 tbsp) butter
50g (¼ cup) sugar
zest of 1 orange
14g (5 tsp) instant dry yeast
2 small eggs
200ml (scant 1 cup) water

Sugar Glaze (page 191)

RASPBERRY ICING
200g (2 cups) icing (confectioners') sugar
1 tsp softened butter
5 tsp warm water
few drops of raspberry extract and pink food colouring

CREAM FILLING
200ml (scant 1 cup) fresh cream
20g (¼ cup) icing (confectioners') sugar
¼ tsp vanilla extract

100g (¼ cup) raspberry jam

Place all dough ingredients in a large mixing bowl. Using a wooden spoon, combine to form a dough. Tip dough out onto a lightly floured surface and knead for 15–20 minutes, resting for 30 seconds every 3–4 minutes, until dough is smooth and elastic. This will take a while; the dough will be sticky to the touch. Don't be tempted to add excessive amounts of flour during the kneading process – just persevere with the softness.

Place dough in a lightly oiled large bowl, cover with clingfilm (plastic wrap) and leave in a warm place for 45 minutes, until it has almost doubled in size.

Tip dough out onto work surface. Gently deflate by folding it onto itself three or four times, then return dough to the bowl, cover with clingfilm (plastic wrap) and leave in a warm place for a further 30 minutes.

Tip dough out onto a lightly floured work surface and divide it into 12 pieces, each about 70g (2½oz). Roll each piece into a ball and shape into a finger about 13cm (5in) long. Place dough fingers on a baking tray (cookie sheet) lined with baking (parchment) paper, leaving room for them to double in size. Cover with clingfilm (plastic wrap) and set aside in a warm place for 40 minutes. The finger buns should just touch each other when they've risen.

Just before baking buns, make sugar glaze and set aside.

When buns have risen, bake in a preheated 190°C/375°F/Gas 5 oven for 12–15 minutes until light golden brown. Remove from oven and immediately brush with hot sugar glaze. Set on a wire rack to cool.

Make raspberry icing by sifting icing (confectioners') sugar into a bowl. Gradually stir in butter and warm water to form a thick paste, adding more water or icing (confectioners') sugar if necessary. Add raspberry extract and food colouring a few drops at a time for a pretty pink colour.

Once the finger buns have cooled, separate them from each other. Dip the top of each finger bun into the icing. Smooth it with your finger, then leave to set on a wire rack.

Make the filling by lightly whipping cream with sugar and vanilla. Spoon mixture into a piping (pastry) bag fitted with a small star nozzle (tip). Spoon the raspberry jam into another piping (pastry) bag. Using a sharp serrated knife, slice each iced bun down the middle, not all the way through, leaving about 5mm (¼in) intact at the bottom. Open up the split and pipe a thin line of raspberry jam in the bottom of the bun, then pipe a generous spiral of whipped cream into the middle of each finger. Finally, pipe a spot of raspberry jam on top.

VARIATION: For chocolate icing, add 1½ tablespoons of cocoa powder to the icing (confectioners') sugar and omit the raspberry extract and colouring.

Cinnamon & Raisin Toast Bread

There is only one way to eat this bread: slice in super-thick slices (2–2.5cm/¾–1in), toast, then smear with whipped butter. Oh man, it's just so, so good. You'll probably need to make two loaves, because it won't last long! Make sure you soak the raisins overnight to get them nice and plump, and take care when kneading them into the dough at the final stages.

MAKES 1 x 500G (1LB 2OZ) LOAF

DOUGH
150g (1 cup) raisins
300g (2 cups) strong bread flour
5g (1 tsp) salt
25g (2 tbsp) butter
25g (2 tbsp) sugar
7g (2½ tsp) instant dry yeast
10g (3 tsp) ground cinnamon
1 small egg
150ml (⅔ cup) water

40g (3 tbsp) cold butter, cut into
4 x 5mm (¼in) cubes
30g (2 tbsp) melted butter, for
glazing loaf after baking

A day in advance, toss the raisins in 50ml (scant ¼ cup) hot water and leave to soak overnight.

The next day, place all the dough ingredients except the plumped raisins in a large mixing bowl. Using a wooden spoon, combine to form a dough. Tip dough out onto a lightly floured surface and knead for 15 minutes, resting it for 1 minute every 2–3 minutes, until dough is smooth and elastic. This will take a while; the dough will be sticky to the touch at first, but don't be tempted to add excessive amounts of flour during the kneading process – just persevere with the softness. Add the raisins and continue to knead very gently, taking care not to smash them, until they are incorporated into the dough.

Lightly oil a bowl large enough to allow dough to double in bulk. Put dough in bowl, cover with clingfilm (plastic wrap) and leave in a warm place for 45 minutes.

Gently knock back dough in the bowl by folding it back onto itself; this will deflate it slightly, but it will develop more strength. Cover again with clingfilm (plastic wrap) and leave for 30 minutes.

Grease a 500g (1lb 2oz) loaf tin (pan).

Tip dough out onto a lightly floured work surface, flatten and mould into a rectangular loaf shape (page 36). Place loaf in prepared tin (pan). Cover with clingfilm (plastic wrap) and leave to prove for 1 hour.

Using a sharp knife or razor blade, make a 5mm-(¼in-)deep cut straight down the centre of the loaf and place the four knobs of butter down the length of the cut. Place tin (pan) in a preheated 190–200°C/375–400°F/Gas 5–6 oven and close oven door quickly. Bake for 20–25 minutes until a nice golden brown colour. Remove loaf from oven and brush the surface immediately with melted butter.

When cool, cut into thick slices and toast.

Pain aux Raisins

Pain aux raisins is sometimes made using croissant or Danish pastry dough, but I find that too rich and too flaky. Here I have used a simple brioche dough. The secret is to prepare the dough the night before – this makes it easier to handle and gives it a full fermented flavour. Soaking the raisins the day before makes them nice and plump. If you are not a huge fan of raisins, use chocolate chips instead.

MAKES 12–14 PAIN AUX RAISINS

BRIOCHE DOUGH
500g (3 cups) strong bread flour
10g (2 tsp) salt
50g (¼ cup) sugar
12g (4 tsp) instant dry yeast
60ml (¼ cup) cold water
6 eggs (300g/11oz), at room temperature
200g (scant 1 cup) butter, softened

200g (1¼ cups) raisins
1 egg whisked with a little milk, for egg wash

CRÈME PÂTISSIÈRE
150ml (⅔ cup) whole milk
3 egg yolks
25g (2 tbsp) caster (superfine) sugar
1 tsp vanilla extract with seeds
15g (scant 2 tbsp) cornflour (cornstarch)

APRICOT GLAZE
100g (¼ cup) apricot jam
4 tbsp water

Prepare brioche dough a day in advance. Mix flour, salt, sugar and yeast together in a large bowl. Add water and eggs and, using a wooden spoon, combine to form a dough. Tip dough out onto a lightly floured work surface and knead for at least 8 minutes, until it starts to become strong, elastic and smooth. Add softened butter gradually, in 6–8 additions, while still kneading. The dough will be sticky at first. Knead for 10–15 minutes, resting for 1 minute every 2–3 minutes, until dough is very smooth, elastic, soft and shiny. Place dough in a lightly oiled large bowl, cover with clingfilm (plastic wrap) and leave in a warm place for 1 hour, until it has almost doubled in size.

Tip dough out onto the work surface and gently deflate by folding it onto itself three or four times. Return it to the bowl, cover with clingfilm (plastic wrap) and place in the refrigerator overnight (12 hours). Wash raisins in hot water and drain in a sieve (strainer) overnight. Make the crème pâtissière (see below) and place in the refrigerator overnight.

The next day, line two baking trays (cookie sheets) with baking (parchment) paper. Remove brioche dough from the refrigerator and roll out on a floured work surface to 60cm x 25cm (23in x 10in). Position dough rectangle on work surface with long edge facing you. Using a spatula, spread a 3mm (⅛in) layer of crème pâtissière over the dough, all the way to the edges of the rectangle. Sprinkle plumped raisins on top of crème pâtissière. Roll dough towards you, starting at the top. Keep the roll tight and even. Cut the roll into 3cm-(1¼in-) thick slices. To close the pain aux raisins, tuck the tail of each slice under the dough.

Place pain aux raisins 5cm (2in) apart on prepared trays (sheets). Cover with clingfilm (plastic wrap) and leave to rise at room temperature for about 1 hour, until they have doubled in size and appear light in texture.

Brush pain aux raisins with egg wash. Bake in a preheated 210°C/410°F/Gas 6½ oven for 15–20 minutes, until light golden brown.

Make apricot glaze by placing jam and water in a saucepan and bringing to the boil. Strain through a sieve (strainer). Brush hot apricot glaze over pain aux raisins as soon as they come out of the oven. Allow to cool completely before eating.

CRÈME PÂTISSIÈRE

Place milk in a saucepan and bring to the boil. In a bowl, beat egg yolks with sugar, vanilla and cornflour (cornstarch). Pour the hot milk over the mixture, beating all the time. Return the mixture to the saucepan and bring it back to a simmer over a low heat. Cook the custard for 2–3 minutes, stirring all the time to prevent it from burning. Remove from heat, place in a bowl, cover, and allow to cool completely. Keep in the refrigerator overnight. Before using, whisk until smooth and spreadable.

Swedish Cinnamon Rolls

These little buns are everywhere in Sweden and are one of their national treasures along with cardamom buns. The simplicity of the brown sugar and cinnamon is magical when the sugar caramelises. You can also shape these in a snail shape rather than tie them in a knot. I have added a little ground cardamom to the dough to give it that extra earthiness – it tastes great with the cinnamon. These rolls are perfect with a hot cup of good coffee, and children love them, too.

MAKES 12–14 ROLLS

DOUGH
15g (5 tsp) instant dry yeast
500g (3 cups) strong bread flour
10g (2 tsp) salt
100g (scant ½ cup) butter
75g (generous ⅓ cup) sugar
1 tsp ground cardamom, optional
1 medium egg
260ml (1 cup) milk, at 30°C (86°F)

FILLING
50g (¼ cup) soft brown sugar
5–10g (1½–3 tsp) ground cinnamon

additional flour for dusting
1 egg whisked with 1 tbsp water, for egg wash
50g (2oz) nibbed sugar, optional

In a small bowl, mix yeast, a little milk and some flour together to form a slurry (this helps dissolve the large amount of yeast). Place all dough ingredients, including yeast mixture, in a large mixing bowl. Using a wooden spoon, combine to form a dough.

Tip dough out onto a lightly floured surface and knead for 15 minutes, resting it for 1 minute every 2–3 minutes, until it is smooth and elastic. The dough should not be too soft – it needs to be a little firm to hold its shape. Put dough in a lightly oiled bowl, cover with clingfilm (plastic wrap) and leave in a warm place for 45 minutes.

Tip dough onto the work surface and gently deflate by folding it three or four times onto itself. Return dough to the bowl, cover with clingfilm (plastic wrap) and leave for another 30 minutes.

Line two baking trays (cookie sheets) with baking (parchment) paper. Prepare filling by stirring together sugar and cinnamon.

Tip dough onto a lightly floured work surface and, using a rolling pin, roll out to a 45cm (17in) square. Using a pastry brush, brush dough surface lightly with water, then sprinkle evenly with sugar and cinnamon filling (see image 1). Fold dough in half (see image 2) and then cut into ten 12cm x 2.5cm (5in x 1in) strips. Stretch out a strip and, using your palms, twist it in alternate directions so that the rope is now twisted (see image 3). Tie each twist in a double knot (see image 4). Place twists on prepared baking trays (cookie sheets), tucking loose ends underneath. Cover loosely with clingfilm (plastic wrap) and leave in a warm place for 45–60 minutes.

Brush rolls with egg wash. Sprinkle with nibbed sugar, if you like. Bake in a preheated 190°C/375°F/Gas 5 oven for 15–18 minutes, or until golden brown. Remove from the oven and cool completely on a wire rack.

My Boston Bun

This is an update on my favourite afternoon-tea snack. I have added Chinese five spice. When I was an apprentice at Rangiora Bakery, we used to make spiced Boston buns on Fridays. Enjoy a slice (or two) spread with salted butter, with your favourite cup of tea.

MAKES 3 BOSTON BUNS

PREPARED FRUIT
85g (½ cup) currants

85g (½ cup) sultanas (golden raisins)

DOUGH
300g (scant 2 cups) strong bread flour

5g (1 tsp) salt

25g (2 tbsp) butter

25g (2 tbsp) sugar

zest of 1 orange

7g (2½ tsp) instant dry yeast

1 tsp Chinese five spice

1 small egg

150ml (⅔ cup) water

REAL RASPBERRY ICING
150g (⅔ cup) unsalted butter, softened

150g (1½ cups) icing (confectioners') sugar

50g (scant ½ cup) fresh raspberries (if using frozen, thaw to room temperature first and drain off the liquid)

Sugar Glaze (page 191)

75g (scant 1 cup) shredded coconut, for topping

Prepare dried fruit a day in advance. Wash currants and sultanas (golden raisins) in hot water, drain in a sieve (strainer) and then allow to sit overnight in a covered container to absorb the water and become nice and plump.

Place all dough ingredients in a large mixing bowl. Using a wooden spoon, combine to form a dough. Tip dough onto a lightly floured work surface and knead for 15–20 minutes, resting it for 30 seconds every 3–4 minutes, until dough is smooth and elastic. This will take a while, but don't be tempted to add excessive amounts. Add the prepared fruit and continue to knead very gently until incorporated.

Lightly oil a bowl large enough for dough to double in bulk. Put dough in bowl and cover with clingfilm (plastic wrap). Leave in a warm place for 45 minutes. Gently knock back dough in the bowl. Cover again with clingfilm (plastic wrap) and leave for 30 minutes.

Tip dough out onto a lightly floured work surface, divide into three equal pieces and mould into round balls. Leave to rest for 5–10 minutes. Line two baking trays (cookie sheets) with baking (parchment) paper.

Flatten each dough ball to a 15cm (6in) circle with the palm of your hand. Place at least 5cm (2in) apart on prepared baking trays (cookie sheets). Cover with clingfilm (plastic wrap) and leave to rise for 30–40 minutes, until doubled in size.

While dough is rising, prepare raspberry icing. Place butter and icing (confectioners') sugar in a mixer with a cake beater attachment. Beat until light, creamy and fluffy. Add raspberries and beat again to mix in evenly. Keep icing in a covered container until required. It must be soft for spreading.

Place buns in a preheated 180–190°C/350–375°F/Gas 4–5 oven and bake for approximately 15 minutes, until golden brown, swapping the position of the trays (sheets) halfway through baking. While buns are baking, prepare the sugar glaze (see page 191).

Remove buns from oven and brush them with sugar glaze to give a shiny surface. Leave to cool completely on a wire rack.

Using a palette knife or the back of a spoon, spread raspberry icing in a circular pattern on buns, almost to the edge. Immediately sprinkle with shredded coconut and press to stick to the icing.

NYC Sticky Pecan Buns

I was introduced to these heavenly sticky treats when I was studying at the American Institute of Baking. Caramel, pecans, rich sweet soft bun . . . they are outrageous and so, so decadent. They are just as good on day three as on day one.

MAKES 12 LARGE BUNS

DOUGH

15g (5 tsp) instant dry yeast, mixed to a slurry with a little flour and water
500g (3 cups) strong bread flour
10g (2 tsp) salt
100g (scant ½ cup) butter
75g (generous ⅓ cup) sugar
1 medium egg
260ml (1 cup) milk, at 30°C (86°F)

CINNAMON SUGAR FILLING

45g (scant ¼ cup) sugar
45g (scant ¼ cup) brown sugar
5g (1½ tsp) ground cinnamon

STICKY BUN GLAZE

200g (1 cup) brown sugar
100g (scant ½ cup) butter
pinch of salt
80g (scant ¼ cup) honey
½ tsp vanilla extract
¼ tsp ground cinnamon

120g (scant 1 cup) chopped pecans or walnuts

Place all dough ingredients in a large mixing bowl and, using a wooden spoon, combine to form a dough. Tip dough out onto a lightly floured work surface and knead for 15 minutes, resting it for 1 minute every 2–3 minutes, until it is smooth and elastic. The dough should not be too soft – it needs to be a little firm so that it holds its shape during the folding, twisting and shaping stage. Put it in a lightly oiled bowl, cover with clingfilm (plastic wrap) and leave in a warm place for 45 minutes.

Tip dough onto the work surface and gently deflate by folding it onto itself three or four times, then return it to the bowl, cover with clingfilm (plastic wrap) and leave for another 30 minutes.

While dough is rising, make the sticky bun glaze. Very gently melt all the ingredients together in a saucepan over a low heat until the sugar is dissolved. Do not boil! Grease two 6-hole Texas muffin tins (pans) well with butter or non-stick spray. Place 2 tablespoons (approximately 30g/1¼oz) of sticky bun glaze in the bottom of each muffin hole, then approximately 10g (3 teaspoons) of chopped pecan or walnuts on top.

Mix cinnamon sugar ingredients together in a small bowl.

Tip dough onto a lightly floured work surface. Using a rolling pin, roll out to a 45cm x 35cm (17in x 14in) rectangle. Arrange it so a long edge is facing you. Brush dough lightly with water, then sprinkle cinnamon sugar evenly over, leaving 1cm (½in) free at the bottom long edge. Starting at the top edge, roll dough towards you, keeping the roll tight and even. Seal at the bottom edge. Lengthen the log to 50cm (20in) by rolling it. Using a large chef's knife, cut the roll into 12 even slices, approximately 4cm (1½in) thick. Place each dough piece in a muffin hole, with the spiral cut side sitting on the sticky bun glaze. Cover with clingfilm (plastic wrap) and leave to rise for about 1 hour at room temperature, until doubled in size and light in texture.

When buns have risen, remove clingfilm (plastic wrap) and place trays (sheets) directly into a preheated 200°C/400°F/Gas 6 oven. Bake for 15–20 minutes until light golden brown. Remove from oven. Wait 1 minute, then tip the muffin pan upside down and allow the buns to fall out onto the baking tray (cookie sheet). Be careful – the sticky toffee glaze will be extremely hot! Allow to cool, then serve.

Chocolate Kugelhopf

Kugelhopf is a classic from the Alsace region of France, particularly the town of Strasbourg where it's pretty much their signature product. It has a lovely fermented flavour due to the pre-ferment, which is combined with the creamed batter to make the final dough. It's very light in texture and the chocolate filling makes it extra special and great as an afternoon-tea cake. For this recipe you will need a 750g (26oz) Kugelhopf mould (available from specialty cookware stores).

MAKES 1 LARGE KUGELHOPF

FERMENT
75g (½ cup) strong bread flour
7g (2½ tsp) instant dry yeast
good pinch of sugar
150ml (⅔ cup) milk, tepid

DOUGH
110g (scant ½ cup) butter, softened
70g (⅓ cup) sugar
1 small egg plus 2 egg yolks
300g (scant 2 cups) strong bread flour
5g (1 tsp) salt
1 quantity of Ferment

CHOCOLATE FILLING
60g (¼ cup) fresh cream
130g (4½oz) dark chocolate, finely chopped

icing (confectioners') sugar, for dusting

Make the ferment ahead and rest as required. Place flour, yeast and sugar in a bowl and stir to combine. Pour in milk and, using a wooden spoon, stir all ingredients to give a smooth, lump-free batter. Cover bowl and leave in a warm place to ferment for 20 minutes until it becomes a frothy, spongy batter.

For dough, put butter and sugar in a bowl and, using a wooden spoon, cream together until light and fluffy. Gradually add egg and egg yolks, beating between each addition, until light and fluffy.

In a large bowl, place flour, salt, prepared ferment and creamed egg and sugar mixture. Mix with a wooden spoon until it forms a dough. Turn dough out onto a lightly floured work surface and knead for 15 minutes, resting it for 1 minute every 2–3 minutes, until it is smooth, elastic and a little sticky. The dough will seem very sticky at first, but it will firm up as you knead it. Don't be tempted to add excess flour.

Place dough in a lightly oiled large bowl and cover with clingfilm (plastic wrap). Leave to ferment for 1 hour in a warm place (24–25°C/75–77°F). Gently knock back the dough in the bowl by folding it back on itself; this will deflate it slightly, but it will develop more strength. Mould into a ball and place back in the lightly oiled bowl. Cover and leave to rest for 30 minutes.

While dough is resting, make the chocolate filling. Place cream in a saucepan and bring to the boil. Remove from the heat and add chocolate. Using a wooden spoon, stir until chocolate has melted. Place in a bowl, cover with clingfilm (plastic wrap) and set aside. Use the chocolate filling while it's still warm and spreadable.

Lightly grease a Kugelhopf mould by brushing with melted butter.

Tip dough out onto a lightly floured work surface and flatten it into a rectangle. Using a rolling pin, roll dough to an even 45cm x 25cm (17in x 10in) rectangle, 4–5mm (⅙–¼in) thick. This will take some time: be patient, and allow dough to relax for a few minutes when rolling becomes difficult.

Position dough rectangle with long edge facing you. Using a palette knife, spread chocolate filling evenly over dough rectangle, leaving a 1cm (½in) gap at the bottom edge. Lightly moisten this edge with water. Starting at the top, roll the long edge downwards to form a Swiss-(jelly-) roll shape. Make the Kugelhopf roll a bit longer, to fit in the mould, by rolling it lightly on the work surface. Join the two ends of the roll together to form a ring shape. Place the dough ring seam-side up into the prepared Kugelhopf mould, then cover with clingfilm (plastic wrap) and leave in a warm place for approximately 1½ hours, until almost doubled in size.

Place mould on tray (sheet) in a preheated 180–190°C/350–375°F/ Gas 4–5 oven and bake for 30–40 minutes. If the top surface is becoming too dark, place a sheet of greaseproof (wax) paper over the top during the final stages of baking. Allow to cool in the mould for 10 minutes before tipping out onto a wire rack. Leave to cool completely, then dust with icing (confectioners') sugar.

Blueberry & Cranberry Bagels

The boiling process gives bagels that characteristic chewy outer texture and dense inner crumb. The dried cranberries and blueberries add a sweetness and tartness combined. Try these with cream cheese and raspberry jam for a berry sensation.

MAKES 10 BAGELS

DOUGH
500g (3 cups) strong bread flour
10g (2 tsp) salt
15g (1 tbsp) soft brown sugar
5g (1¼ tsp) instant dry yeast
15ml (1 tbsp) olive oil
300ml (1¼ cups) chilled water
75g (⅔ cup) dried blueberries
75g (⅔ cup) dried cranberries

200g (1¼ cups) coarse semolina or polenta (cornmeal), to sprinkle on baking tray (cookie sheet)
2 tbsp liquid honey, to add to boiling water

Line a baking tray (cookie sheet) with baking (parchment) paper, and sprinkle it generously with semolina or polenta (cornmeal).

Place dry ingredients, oil and water in a large mixing bowl. Using your hands, combine to form a very firm dough. Don't be tempted to add any water at this stage, or the bagels will lose their shape while they are being boiled. Tip dough out onto a lightly floured surface. Knead for 10–15 minutes, resting for 30 seconds every 2–3 minutes, until dough is smooth and elastic.

Add blueberries and cranberries and continue to very gently knead until they are incorporated into the dough. Take your time, making sure the dough remains very firm. Don't worry if the berries begin to break up – this will give a marbled effect through the dough.

Immediately cut dough into 10 strips, approximately 90g (3¼oz) each. Roll each dough strip into a 15cm-(6in-)long rope. Wrap a strip around your four fingers, with the two ends meeting together underneath (see images 1 and 2 on page 66). Applying pressure on the work surface, roll to seal the ends, forming a distinctive ring shape. Place bagel rings 2cm (¾in) apart on prepared baking tray (cookie sheet), cover loosely with clingfilm (plastic wrap) and put in the refrigerator overnight (12–16 hours).

The next day, remove bagels from refrigerator and leave to stand at room temperature for 30–45 minutes.

Line a baking tray (cookie sheet) with baking (parchment) paper.

Fill a large saucepan with water, add the honey and bring to the boil over a high heat. With water at full boil, place two or three bagels into the saucepan and blanch for 30 seconds on each side, a total of 1 minute. Using a slotted spoon, gently remove bagels from the boiling water, making sure all the water has drained off. Place bagels semolina-side down onto the lined baking tray (cookie sheet), leaving a 2cm (¾in) space between each bagel.

Bake in a preheated 220°C/425°F/Gas 7 oven for 20–25 minutes or until a shiny golden brown. Remove from oven, place on a wire rack and leave to cool completely.

Tarte Tropézienne

A good friend of mine, Tim Etchells, introduced me to this rich cream-filled cake-cum-tart when I was filming a TV series and staying at his holiday home in L'Escalet, 10 minutes' drive from Saint Tropez. It was made famous by Brigitte Bardot in 1957: when she starred in the controversial film *And God Created Woman*, she ordered this tart from the Polish baker Alexandre Micka in Saint Tropez every day while on set. It became known as Tarte Tropézienne. This tart is best kept in the refrigerator and will last for several days.

MAKES 1 LARGE TART

BRIOCHE BASE

250g (1½ cups) strong bread flour

5g (1 tsp) salt

25g (2 tbsp) sugar

5g (1¼ tsp) instant dry yeast

30ml (2 tbsp) cold water

3 eggs (150g/5oz when cracked), lightly whisked then chilled

125g (½ cup) butter, softened

Crème Pâtissière (page 192)
Swiss Buttercream (page 192)

1 egg whisked with 1 tbsp water, for egg wash

50g (2oz) nibbed sugar, optional

zest of 2 oranges

150g (⅔ cup) freshly whipped cream

icing (confectioners') sugar, for dusting (optional)

Begin making the brioche base a day in advance. Mix together flour, salt, sugar and yeast in a large bowl. Add the water and three-quarters of the whisked egg. Using a wooden spoon, combine to form a dough.

Tip dough out onto a lightly floured surface and knead for approximately 5 minutes. Gradually add remaining egg in small additions while kneading, until dough starts to become strong, elastic and smooth. Add softened butter in five lots while still kneading. The dough will be sticky at first. Knead for 10–15 minutes, resting it for 30 seconds every 3–4 minutes, until it is very smooth, elastic, soft and shiny. Place dough in a lightly oiled large bowl, cover with clingfilm (plastic wrap) and leave in a warm place for 1 hour, until almost doubled in size.

Tip dough onto the work surface and gently deflate by folding it onto itself three or four times. Return it to the bowl, cover with clingfilm (plastic wrap) and place in the refrigerator overnight (12 hours).

Make the crème pâtissière and the Swiss buttercream, and place in the refrigerator until required.

The next day, remove dough from refrigerator, tip it out onto a floured work surface and mould it into a round ball. Leave to rest on the work surface for 10–15 minutes.

Line a baking tray (cookie sheet) with baking (parchment) paper. Using a rolling pin, roll dough out to a 20cm (8in) circle. Place on tray (sheet), cover with clingfilm (plastic wrap) and leave to prove for approximately 45–60 minutes, until it is nice and puffy.

Brush risen brioche base all over with egg wash. Sprinkle with nibbed sugar, if you like. Bake in a preheated 190°C/375°F/Gas 5 oven for 20–25 minutes or until golden brown. Remove from the oven and cool completely.

Meanwhile, prepare the cream filling. Add orange zest to buttercream and beat until light and fluffy. In a separate bowl, beat the crème pâtissière until smooth, fold in the buttercream until evenly mixed throughout, then fold in the whipped cream.

Once brioche base is cool, slice it in half horizontally. Spoon cream filling onto bottom layer, then replace top layer. Place in the refrigerator for a few hours to firm up the filling.

Remove tart from refrigerator at least half an hour before serving. If you haven't sprinkled nibbed sugar over, dust top of tart instead with icing (confectioners') sugar. Slice into wedges to serve.

Jason's Hundreds & Thousands Iced Buns

My son Jason grew up on these little finger buns (he still loves them, even now he's eighteen). He used to pick off the icing, lick the bun clean and then eat the bread. I did my best to get him to take big mouthfuls of the whole bun at once, but he wouldn't have it!

MAKES 12 FINGER BUNS

500g (3 cups) strong bread flour
10g (2 tsp) salt
50g (4 tbsp) butter
50g (¼ cup) sugar
15g (5 tsp) instant dry yeast
2 small eggs
200ml (scant 1 cup) water

Sugar Glaze (page 191)

WHITE ICING
200g (1 cup) icing (confectioners') sugar
1 tsp softened butter
5 tsp warm water

150g (5oz) hundreds and thousands (colored sprinkles), for topping

Place all dough ingredients in a large mixing bowl. Using a wooden spoon, combine to form a dough. Tip dough out onto a lightly floured surface and knead for 15–20 minutes, resting it for 30 seconds every 3–4 minutes, until dough is smooth and elastic. This will take a while; the dough will be sticky to the touch at first, but don't be tempted to add excessive amounts of flour during the kneading process – just persevere with the softness.

Place dough in a lightly oiled large bowl, cover with clingfilm (plastic wrap) and leave in a warm place for 45 minutes, until almost doubled in size.

Tip dough out onto a work surface. Gently deflate it by folding it onto itself three or four times, then return dough to the bowl, cover with clingfilm (plastic wrap) and leave in a warm place for a further 30 minutes.

Tip dough out onto a lightly floured work surface and divide into 12 pieces, about 70g (2½oz) each. Roll each piece into a ball and shape into a finger about 13cm (5in) long. Line a baking tray (cookie sheet) with baking (parchment) paper. Place dough fingers on the tray (sheet), leaving space for them to double in size. Cover with clingfilm (plastic wrap) and set aside in a warm place for 40 minutes. The fingers should just touch each other when they've risen.

Preheat oven to 190°C/375°F/Gas 5. Make sugar glaze.

Bake buns for 12–15 minutes, until light golden brown. Remove from oven and immediately brush with hot sugar glaze, then set on a wire rack to cool. When cool, separate the buns.

Make white icing by sifting icing (confectioners') sugar into a bowl. Gradually stir in butter and warm water to form a thick paste. Adjust icing by adding more water or icing (confectioners') sugar if necessary. Put hundreds and thousands onto a plate.

Dip the top of the cooled fingers into the icing, smoothing it with your finger, then dip immediately into the hundreds and thousands (colored sprinkles). Leave on a wire rack to set before serving.

Basic Recipes

Sourdough Levain Starter

This sourdough starter is a bubbly, yeasty batter that will give your bread character and a life of its own: a moist, open texture, nutty fermented flavour and a reddish crust. If you want to make a rye levain starter, replace the strong bread flour with rye flour throughout this recipe. Note that the dough will be stiffer because rye flour absorbs more water.

Days one and two: capturing the wild yeast

You will need:
400g (scant 2½ cups) strong bread flour
500ml (2 cups) water, at about 25°C (77°F)
1 large bowl (preferably glass)
1 piece of muslin cloth (cheesecloth)

On day one, place flour and water in the bowl and mix together to form a smooth batter. Cover with the muslin (cheesecloth) and place the bowl somewhere outside where it will get plenty of fresh air but no direct sunlight. In winter, place it in the warmest part of the house with an occasional breath of fresh air. On day two, after 24 hours, some bubbles may appear on the surface – this is a good sign. Use a wooden spoon to beat air into the mixture, then cover with muslin (cheesecloth) and leave for another 24 hours.

Days three and four: breeding the yeast

There should be bubbles appearing on the surface of the mixture. Start to build on the small amount of wild yeast present by feeding the starter.

You will need:
water, at about 25°C (77°F)
strong bread flour

On day three, pour 200ml (scant 1 cup) water in the bowl and break up the culture in the water. Add 200g (1¼ cups) flour and mix well. Cover the bowl with the muslin (cheesecloth) and let it stand in a warm place. Leave the starter about 24 hours before feeding it again with the same quantities of water and flour.

Days five and six: concentrating the yeast

You will need:
water, at about 25°C (77°F)
strong bread flour

As the wild yeast spores multiply they start getting through their food a bit quicker, so you need to feed them more regularly. About 12 hours after the last feeding on day four, pour off half of the culture and discard. Feed the remainder with 200ml (scant 1 cup) water and 200g (1¼ cups) flour. After 12 hours, feed the culture the same quantities again. On day six, pour off half of the culture and feed twice, as you did on day five.

Day seven and beyond: keeping the yeast alive

This is where having a sourdough starter becomes a bit like owning a pet. Like a pet, yeast needs to be fed three times a day if it is to thrive and do its job well.

You will need:
starter container and lid with a small airhole
rubber spatula (or your hands)

First feed of the day:
100g (3½oz) starter (discard the rest)
50g (⅓ cup) strong bread flour
50ml (scant ¼ cup) water, at about 25°C (77°F)

Allow to ferment for about 8 hours.

Second feed of the day:
200g (7oz) starter
100g (⅔ cup)strong bread flour
100ml (scant ½ cup) water, at about 25°C (77°F)

Allow to ferment for about 8 hours.

Third feed of the day
400g (14oz) starter
200g (scant 2½ cups) strong bread flour
200ml (scant 1 cup) water, at about 25°C (77°F)

Allow the starter to ferment for 8 hours, then start again with the first feed. After a couple of weeks, if all has gone well, you should have a happy and healthy sourdough starter living in your home, as a new member of the family. From about day 10 it will be strong enough to make bread, and its strength will increase as it matures. As your starter ages it will develop consistency, balance and, to a certain extent, immunity from foreign invaders such as bacteria.

The feeding schedule

The timing of your feeding schedule can be organised to suit your day and your baking plans. I prefer to make my dough first thing in the morning, so my feeding schedule looks something like this with only two feeds a day:

8 am the day before baking	first feed
8 pm the day before baking	second feed
8 am on baking day	make dough

If you are just maintaining your starter but not planning to make bread, throwing out nearly a kilo (2¼lb)of starter every day is quite wasteful. Once your starter is bubbling along in a healthy way (at least 2 weeks after day one), it can hibernate in the refrigerator while you are not using it. If you want to do this, do so after the first feed so the yeast has some food to carry it through the hibernation. In the refrigerator, most of the wild yeast will become dormant – snoozing until you wake them up. As time goes on, though, these dormant spores will start to die off. So even while in cold storage, the starter will still need the occasional feed. Once a week is sufficient, using the same amounts as for normal feeding (discarding the excess as required), but you will need to use slightly warmer water (about 35°C/95°F). This will allow the yeast a quick feed before going dormant in the cold again.

A word of warning: you will need to get the starter back on two to three feeds a day at room temperature for at least two days before you can bake with it again. If you try to make bread with starter straight from the refrigerator, you will fail.

How much to feed a starter?

The amount of water and flour fed to a sourdough starter once it is healthy varies from baker to baker. The feeding amounts below are a good guide. The amount of healthy sourdough starter can vary, but the formula should stay the same. As a rule, the total weight of the starter should be fed with half its volume of water and half its volume of flour.

Example:
250g (9oz) healthy sourdough starter
+ 125ml (½ cup) water
+ 125g (¾ cup) flour
= 500g (1lb 2oz) new sourdough starter

Quick Rye Sourdough

25g (¼ cup) strong bread flour
25g (¼ cup) rye flour (coarsely ground or stoneground is best)
30g (2 tbsp) natural unsweetened yoghurt
20ml (4 tsp) warm water
⅛ tsp instant dry yeast

Place all ingredients in a small bowl and mix with a wooden spoon until evenly mixed. Cover and leave to ferment for 12–16 hours, then feed with:

25g (scant ¼ cup) strong bread flour
25g (¼ cup) rye flour
50ml (scant ¼ cup) cold water

Mix with a wooden spoon until evenly mixed. Cover and leave to ferment for another 12 hours.

You now have 200g (7oz) rye sourdough. Use 100g (3½oz) for the recipe, and keep 100g (3½oz) in the container and feed again with the above amounts. Remember you can keep the sourdough in the refrigerator in a covered container and feed it every 10 days or so. Bring it out a day before it is required and feed it twice to make it healthy and strong for using.

Hot Cross Bun Spice Mixture

2 tsp each: ground nutmeg, ginger and coriander
4 tsp each: ground cloves, cinnamon and Chinese five spice

Mix all ingredients together and store in an airtight container. Use as required.

Sugar Glaze

100ml (scant ½ cup) water
50g (¼ cup) sugar
zest of 1 orange
¼ tsp powdered gelatine

Put all ingredients except gelatine into a small saucepan and heat until boiling. Remove from the heat, whisk in the gelatine until dissolved and set aside to use once buns are baked. Alternatively, heat in a microwave oven.

White Icing

220g (scant 2¼ cups) icing (confectioners') sugar
½ tsp butter, softened
zest and juice of 1 lemon

Sift icing (confectioners') sugar into a bowl, add softened butter and zest. Mix with enough lemon juice (approximately 1 tablespoon) to give a spreading or piping consistency.

Vanilla White Icing

25g (2 tbsp) butter
45g (3 tbsp) cream
1 tsp vanilla extract with seeds
150g (1½ cups) icing (confectioners') sugar

Place all ingredients in a saucepan and gently melt together over a low heat, stirring with a wooden spoon or spatula. Use while warm.

Apricot Glaze

150g (scant ½ cup) apricot jam
75ml (5 tbsp) water

Mix apricot jam and water in a saucepan and bring to the boil. Remove from heat and pass through a sieve (strainer) to remove any lumps. Use while hot. Can be reheated in a microwave oven, if necessary.

Almond Cream

50g (4 tbsp) butter, softened
50g (¼ cup) sugar
1 large egg, slightly warmed
50g (½ cup) ground almonds
10g (1¼ tbsp) plain (all-purpose) flour
a few drops of almond extract

Beat butter and sugar together with a wooden spoon until light and creamy. Add egg gradually to avoid curdling, and beat in well. Add ground almonds, flour and almond extract. Mix for a few minutes to a smooth, creamy consistency.

Crème Pâtissière (Pastry Cream)

250ml (1 cup) whole milk
4 egg yolks
50g (¼ cup) sugar
30g (¼ cup) cornflour (cornstarch)

Put milk in a saucepan and bring to the boil. In a bowl, beat egg yolks together with sugar and cornflour (cornstarch). Pour hot milk over the egg mixture, beating all the time. Return the mixture to the saucepan and bring it to a simmer, stirring all the time. Remove from the heat and allow to cool. Keep in a covered container in the refrigerator until needed. Whisk before using.

Swiss Buttercream

170g (scant 1 cup) caster (superfine) sugar
2 egg whites, at room temperature
225g (1 cup) butter, at room temperature

Using a hand whisk, whisk sugar and egg whites together in a double boiler until sugar has dissolved and the temperature reaches 50°C (122°F) on a candy thermometer (make sure it is not over 50°C (122°F), or it will cook the eggs). Whisk the mixture to a soft peak meringue using an electric mixer, then beat in the butter, a little at a time, until fully incorporated and the buttercream is light and fluffy. Cover until needed.

Cream Chantilly

200ml (scant 1 cup) fresh cream
25g (2 tbsp) caster (superfine) sugar
1 tsp vanilla extract with seeds

Place all ingredients in a bowl and whisk until soft or stiff peaks form, depending on the required consistency. Cover and place in the refrigerator until required. You may need to whip again before serving.

Caramelised Onion

2 tbsp olive oil
2 large onions, cut in half then sliced thinly
1 tbsp brown sugar
good pinch of ground nutmeg
salt and pepper to taste

In a frying pan (skillet), heat olive oil until hot, add onion and brown sugar and cook over a medium heat for a few minutes to allow onion to soften. Reduce heat to low and slowly cook for around 30 minutes, stirring from time to time. Remove from heat and season with nutmeg, salt and pepper. Place in a bowl and set aside to cool.

Decorating Dough

200g (scant 1¼ cups) strong bread flour
¼ tsp salt
20g (1½ tbsp) butter, softened
85ml (⅓ cup) water

Place all ingredients in a large mixing bowl. Using a wooden spoon, combine to form a dough. Tip dough out onto a work surface and knead by hand for approximately 7–8 minutes. This dough is very firm – don't be tempted to add any more water! Place in a plastic bag until required, to prevent it from drying out. This decorating dough must be made in advance and will keep for at least 1 day at room temperature or 2 days in the refrigerator.

Homemade Raspberry Jam

MAKES 3 x 200ML (7OZ) JARS
450g (3¾ cups) raspberries
450g (2¼ cups) sugar

To sterilise jars, place three thoroughly clean 200ml (7oz) jars on their side in a preheated 170°C/340°F/Gas 3 oven for 10 minutes. Then turn oven off and leave jars inside until jam is ready to pot. Place two or three saucers in the freezer to chill.

Rinse the raspberries. Place in a large saucepan and cook over a gentle heat for 2–3 minutes until juice is just beginning to run. Add sugar and stir over a gentle heat for 1–2 minutes until sugar has dissolved. Increase the heat and bring to a vigorous boil. Boil for 5–10 minutes.

Remove from the heat and test jam by daubing a little on one of the chilled saucers. Cool for a few seconds, then push the jam with your fingertip. If it wrinkles, it has reached setting point. If not, continue to boil for a further 2 minutes, then test again.

When setting point is reached, pour jam into jars. Cover the surface with a disc of waxed paper and seal with a lid. Label and store in a cool dark place for up to 3 months.

Weights, Measures & Temperatures

Quantities in this book are given in metric and American (spoon and cup) measures.

Standard spoon and cup measurements used are: 1 teaspoon = 5ml, 1 tablespoon = 15ml, 1 cup = 250ml. All measures given are level unless otherwise stated.

ounces (oz) to grams (g):
Conversion: 1oz = 28.4g
Example: 16oz x 28.4g = 454.4g

pounds (lb) to kilograms (kg):
Conversion: 1lb (16oz) = 454g
Example: 1lb 3oz (19oz) x 28.4g = 0.539kg

Celsius (°C) to Fahrenheit (°F):
Formula: °F − 32 ÷ 9 x 5 = °C
Example: 425°F − 32 ÷ 9 x 5 = 218°C

Fahrenheit (°F) to Celsius (°C):
Formula: °C ÷ 5 x 9 + 32 = °F
Example: 220°C ÷ 5 x 9 + 32 = 428°F

Liquid and volume measures		
Metric	**Imperial**	**American**
5ml	⅙ fl oz	1 tsp
10ml	⅓ fl oz	1 dsp
15ml	½ fl oz	1 tbsp
60ml	2 fl oz	¼ cup (4 tbsp)
85ml	2½ fl oz	⅓ cup
90ml	3 fl oz	⅜ cup (6 tbsp)
125ml	4 fl oz	½ cup
180ml	6 fl oz	¾ cup
250ml	8 fl oz	1 cup
300ml	10 fl oz (½ pint)	1¼ cups
375ml	12 fl oz	1½ cups
435ml	14 fl oz	1¾ cups
500ml	16 fl oz	2 cups (1 pint)
600ml	20 fl oz (1 pint)	2¼ cups
750ml	24 fl oz	3 cups
1 litre	32 fl oz	4 cups
1.25 litres	40 fl oz (2 pints)	5 cups
1.5 litres	48 fl oz	6 cups
2.5 litres	80 fl oz (4 pints)	10 cups

Dry measures

Metric	Imperial
30g	1oz
45g	1½oz
55g	2oz
70g	2½oz
85g	3oz
100g	3½oz
110g	4oz
125g	4½oz
140g	5oz
280g	10oz
450g	16oz (1lb)
500g	1lb 2oz
700g	1½lb
800g	1¾lb
1 kilogram	2¼lb
1.5 kilograms	3lb 4½oz
2 kilograms	4lb 6oz

Length

Metric	Imperial
0.5cm	¼ inch
1cm	½ inch
1.5cm	¾ inch
2.5cm	1 inch

Oven temperature equivalents

Gas mark	°F	°C	
¼	212	100	Very Cool
½	265	130	Very Cool
1	290	145	Very Cool
2	310	155	Cool
3	340	170	Warm
4	350	180	Moderate or Medium
5	375	195	Moderately Hot or Medium Hot
6	400	205	Moderately Hot or Medium Hot
7	425	220	Hot
8	450	230	Hot
9	475	240	Very Hot
10	500	250	Very Hot

The temperatures given in recipes in this book are the approximate temperature at the centre of the oven. Temperatures in °C have been rounded up or down to the nearest 10°C.

Formulas

Bakers tend to talk about 'formulas' rather than 'recipes'. If this sounds more like a chemistry lab than a kitchen or a baking facility, it is because a bakery is very much like a chemistry laboratory both in the scientific accuracy of the procedures and in the complex reactions that take place during the mixing procedure and the baking cycle. In fact, in France the pâtisseries are often called laboratories.

Scaling ingredients

All ingredients must be weighed accurately. Water, milk and beaten eggs may be measured by volume. They are scaled at 1 kilogram per litre (2¼lb per 4 cups); for example, 1kg (2¼lb) water = 1 litre (4 cups) water. If quantities are large, it is advisable to weigh these ingredients on an accurate set of scales.

Recipe balance

Recipes are balanced formulations: if you add too much of one ingredient, this will upset another ingredient and cause an imbalance in the recipe. Special care must be taken when weighing salt, baking powder, spices, sugar and other ingredients used in small amounts. Often, the smaller the amount, the more effect it will have on the finished baked product.

Bakers' percentages

Bakers use a simple but versatile system of percentages for expressing their formulas or recipes. Bakers' percentages indicate the quantities of each item that would be required if 100 kilograms (1.75 quarts) of flour was used. In other words, each ingredient is expressed as a percentage of the total flour weight.

The percentage of each ingredient is its total weight divided by the weight of the flour, multiplied by 100.

For example:

$$\frac{\text{Total weight of ingredient}}{\text{Total weight of flour}} \quad x \quad 100 \quad = \quad \% \text{ of ingredient}$$

The flour is always expressed as 100%. If two kinds of flour are used, their total is still 100%.

Any ingredient that weighs the same as the flour is also expressed as 100%.

See the following recipe to help understand how these percentages are used. Check the figures using the above equation to make sure you understand them.

Basic White Bread

Ingredient	Weight	%
Bread flour	1000g (2¼lb)	100
Salt	20g (¾oz)	2
Sugar	10g (⅓oz)	1
Oil	30ml (1fl oz)	3
Instant dry yeast	10g (⅓oz)	1
Water	650ml (scant 3 cups)	65
Total weight	1720g (3.79lb)	
Yield @ 100g per roll	17.2 rolls (rounded to 17 rolls)	

Glossary

Not all the terms explained in this glossary appear in this book, but I have included them to help the baker understand the terminology commonly used in baking.

Aerate – incorporate air or carbon dioxide gas during one or more stages of the production of bakery products. Aeration allows the baked product to become light and airy. Air can be introduced by whisking, beating or mixing. Carbon dioxide gas can be introduced by either baking powder or yeast.

Baking temperature – the term used when baking in an oven at correctly controlled temperatures, expressed here in degrees Celsius (°C), Farenheit (°F) and Gas mark.

Baking time – how long you bake your product in an oven at correctly controlled temperatures.

Bloom – term used to indicate a healthy shine or sparkle on baked goods.

Bread flour – strong flour milled from hard wheat, which has a high protein content and is generally used for the production of yeast goods.

Bulk fermentation – the period of time that a yeasted dough is left to ferment in bulk.

Bun wash – a liquid, usually sugar and water boiled together, which is brushed on yeast buns immediately on removal from the oven to achieve a glaze or shine.

Cake flour – (often referred to as plain (all-purpose) flour or soft flour) soft flour milled from soft wheat, which has a low to medium protein content and is generally used for the production of cakes and sometimes biscuits and cookies. Not ideal for bread baking.

Caramelisation – the browning effect when sugar is heated.

Carbon dioxide, CO_2 – the gas produced by baking powder or yeast fermentation that aerates baked goods.

Coagulate – setting of a protein by heating, e.g. gluten in flour is set by baking.

Crème pâtissière – a thick custard containing eggs, milk, sugar, vanilla and flour, also called pastry cream.

Decorate – adding seeds, fruits, nuts, chocolate or icing to embellish the bakery product; or making decorative cuts or slashes in the top of the baked product.

Develop – thoroughly mixing a dough to increase the elasticity and extensibility of the gluten (protein in flour).

Divide – (or scale) the process of dividing dough into portions by size or weight before shaping and baking.

Dock – to pierce or prick pastry before baking, to allow steam to escape and to avoid blistering.

Dough – a mixture of flour and liquid combined with yeast or not.

Dust – to sprinkle flour or similar onto a work surface to prevent the dough or paste from sticking.

Dust (to decorate) – sprinkle icing (confectioners') sugar or flour through a fine-mesh sieve (strainer) over baked products to decorate.

Egg wash – beaten egg, usually diluted with water or milk, brushed onto baked goods to achieve a glazed surface.

Emulsion – a uniform mixture of two substances or ingredients that don't normally mix together (e.g. fats and eggs in a cake batter), usually assisted by an emulsifier (e.g. the lecithin in the egg).

Ferment – a mixture of water or milk, yeast and flour that is allowed to ferment at controlled temperatures and times, for use in yeasted dough.

Fermentation – the process by which yeast changes carbohydrates into carbon dioxide and alcohol. This gas causes aeration in fermented yeast products, and the alcohol adds flavour.

Firm/tight dough – a dough containing less or insufficient liquids.

Gelatinisation – starch heated with water to form a thick jelly-type paste upon cooling.

Glaze – a shiny coating such as a syrup, apricot jam or egg wash applied to bakery products before or after baking.

Gliadin – an extensible protein found in wheat that combines with another protein, glutenin, to form gluten.

Gluten – an elastic insoluble substance formed by the two proteins gliadin and glutenin present in wheat, which, when mixed with liquid, gives structure and strength to baked products.

Glutenin – an elastic protein found in wheat that combines with gliadin to form gluten.

High grade flour – see Strong flour.

Intermediate proof – (also referred to as 'first proof', 'recovery time' or 'resting time') a resting period of 10–15 minutes between rounding and final make-up or shaping of a yeasted bread dough; it allows the gluten network to relax.

Knock back – during the bulk fermentation period of a yeasted dough, it increases in volume (often to double) because of the gases given off by the yeast. To avoid the gases escaping prematurely, the dough is gently 'knocked back' by very gently pushing and folding the dough, usually three-quarters of the way through the bulk fermentation period.

Lamination – forming a number of layers of fat and dough, as when making puff pastry, Danish pastries or croissants.

Lean dough – a yeasted dough low in fat and sugar.

Levain starter – wild yeast spores captured from the air, combined with flour and water and allowed to ferment, then mixed with more flour and other ingredients to make a sourdough or pain au levain bread dough.

Malt flour – a flour made from sprouted wheat or barley. Malt products are an important food source for yeast in yeast-raised doughs. Enzyme-active malt flour is best.

Marzipan – a mixture of ground almonds and sugar, mixed together with sufficient egg to form a firm, pliable paste.

Mould – to shape a piece of dough.

No-time dough – a bread dough made using a larger quantity of yeast and a shorter fermentation time, usually in conjunction with a specific bread improver with vitamin C, specific enzymes, emulsifiers, enzyme-active malt flour, flavour enhancers, etc.

Old dough – a dough that has been over-fermented; can be used in a fresh dough to increase the flavour profile.

Oven spring – the rise of a yeasted dough in the oven due to the expansion of gases caused by oven heat.

Pain au levain – a classic French bread made with a natural yeast starter (levain), salt, flour and water.

Prove – the action of yeast producing carbon dioxide that causes dough to rise.

Prover – a cabinet in which yeasted goods are placed to prove before baking; the prover provides the necessary warm and humid environment.

Resting time – the time required for doughs and pastries to relax after intensive mixing or handling. This is an important step, as it often allows the next stage of production to flow smoothly without causing stress on the product.

Retarding – refrigerating of a yeasted dough to slow the fermentation down, resulting in additional flavour, structure and eating quality.

Rounding up – a method of moulding a piece of dough into a round ball with a smooth skin or surface.

Slack dough – a dough containing excess liquids, making it soft to the feel.

Sourdough – a yeasted dough made with a sponge or starter that has fermented until it has become sour and acidic in taste and flavour. Also the baked loaf, e.g. San Francisco sourdough.

Sponge – a batter or dough of yeast, flour and water that is allowed to ferment and is then mixed with more flour and other ingredients to make a bread dough.

Strong flour – a flour milled from hard wheat, which has a high protein content and is generally used for the production of yeasted goods. Also known as high grade flour, bread flour or strong bread flour.

Yield – the number of units or portions expected out of a recipe, based on a predetermined size or weight.

Acknowledgements

Aaron McLean – you are a great photographer and put up with a lot from behind that lens! What else can I say. . .Check Aaron out at www.aaronmclean.com

Thank you to Kate Stockman, Debra Millar and the team at Penguin New Zealand. As always, it's great to work with such a talented team of professionals.

A big thank you to my team at Baker & Cook for helping bring my artisan bakery vision to reality every single day. I love working with people who love to learn – and you are a great team of people!

Thanks also to Gauri, Anders and Alex for all the support and for keeping my passion alive in everything we do at Baker & Cook (www.bakerandcook.biz).

To the team at Zarbo in Newmarket, Auckland, thank you for allowing Aaron and me to take over your microbakery to bake all the great breads for this book.

As usual, thanks to Air New Zealand. Mike Tod and his team are great supporters and partners in everything that I do globally. Air New Zealand flew me many miles so I could complete this book for you to enjoy, and they have also supported many of my TV series – such a special airline.

To Julie Christie, Georgina Sinclair, Gail Wilson-Waring, Greg Heathcote and the exceptional team at Food TV who work behind the scenes on the baking shows I get involved with. Your vision to bring baking to the forefront goes side by side with my passion.

Paul Hansen – a trusted friend and passionate baker, mentor to many and good all-round nice guy. I often wonder what a baking book written by yourself would be like. Thank you for the wonderful research on the history of bread; it's a complicated, long history but you have captured it perfectly.

Thanks to Jocelyn McCallum and the team behind Pams products and baking ingredients available at New World and Pak'nSave supermarkets in New Zealand. It's always great to use quality baking ingredients you can trust and rely on. You are great supporters of my brand and everything I do in my global baking life.

Lastly I want to thank all the great people out there who, like myself, indulge in all things baking. Without you all, my TV shows and books would not be the success they are. I love getting emails and comments on how well you are all baking using the recipes and tips I provide.

Bake well, and thank you!
Global Baker Dean Brettschneider

Index

About the Author

Dean Brettschneider is a professional baker, pâtissier and entrepreneur. Arguably one of the world's best bakers, with an international following, Dean is truly a global baker. He resides in Denmark, Singapore and New Zealand, where he heads up his global baking empire. He travels regularly and consults in Europe to the baking industry and to many large retailers. Dean is also the founder and co-owner of the global bakery chain Baker & Cook, which has its flagship store in Singapore: www.bakerandcook.biz.

Dean is the author of 12 award-winning books on baking. He appears as co-host and lead judge on the successful reality TV series *New Zealand's Hottest Home Baker*. He also hosts the *Kiwi Baker* series in Shanghai, France, Singapore and California, as well as many other TV programmes that promote baking excellence.

www.globalbaker.com